MY HOLISTIC TEMPLE

Unifying and healing the physical, mental, spiritual, and metaphysical

Otto and Audric Aurelius

Copyright © 2024 by Audric Aurelius

All rights reserved. No part of this publication may be reproduced, stored in a retrieval system, or transmitted, in any form or by any means without the prior written permission of the publisher, nor be otherwise circulated in any form of binding or cover other than that in which it is published and without a similar condition being imposed on the subsequent purchaser.

Print Edition 1, 2024
ISBN: 9798302098306

Youtube: youtube.com/@AudricAurelius
Enquiries: holisticaudricaurelius@gmail.com

In no way may this text be construed as encouraging or condoning any harmful or illegal act. In no way may this text be construed as able to diagnose, treat, cure or prevent any disease, injury, symptom or condition.

Thank you to our mother and father for all their unconditional help and support.

Thank you to all our friends and communities that supported us and also pushed us to be confident in what we've learned.

Table of Contents

Ch. 1 THE GARDEN OF EDEN..................5
Ch. 2 FASTING = STEM CELLS................20
Ch. 3 DENSITY...................................32
Ch. 4 WATER.....................................40
Ch. 5 FRACTALS.................................58
Ch. 6 TORUS FIELD.............................73
Ch. 7 SPIRITUALITY............................92
Ch. 8 SUN, MOON, AND STARS................103
Ch. 9 GROUNDING...............................126
Ch. 10 THE KEYS TO A GOOD LIFE..........142
Ch. 11 ITS NOT DOOMSDAY....................157
Ch. 12 (1MAD) LIFESTYLE & THE "EZ-28" CHALLENGE......................................161
  APPENDIX: How to 4-day Dry Fast............169

Ch. 1 THE GARDEN OF EDEN

Obviously a story should start with a beginning, and what better beginning than one of the most known beginnings of our current time, the Garden of Eden. Sure it may seem cliché to start from the Garden of Eden, but it will help set the stage for what is to unfold. Before officially beginning, we ask that you exercise good reasoning skills. What we mean by this is to hold and consider a contrarian idea in your mind without throwing it out just because you disagree with it, you cannot have a contrarian opinion until a contrarian thought arises. Ultimately, it is on you the reader to "innerstand" what is being presented and then go search for yourself to truly convince yourself. But everyone must start somewhere, and whether this be where you begin your journey, or furthering along your journey, the synchronicities will tie it all together. And do not forget, we originally started on the same ground as everyone else, through a decade of seeing too many in-consistencies and unlearning and relearning from older ancient texts did we come to the conclusions that we are at now. (Hopefully this can be a step towards changing the indoctrinated foundation for the future.) The saying goes "nothing is new under the sun", and that is exactly the case here, we are merely consolidating old information and bringing it back into the light for all mankind to grow and prosper. This is for posterity. Do not think that anything here is about "one-upping" or "gotch-ya" because a step towards enlightenment for each individual person is a win for all of us together. So, with that said, the Garden of Eden comes from the beginning of the Book of Genesis, and many other beginnings come from there that are also important to mention but we will begin with how God said he placed the stars and luminaries in the firmament, the sky above. (This even comes directly from the chapter of Genesis in the Vatican's bible of all places.) The luminaries being referred to are the Sun and the Moon. Yes we're getting right to it, the sun is a big ball of radium gas that grows and heals life, while the moon is another large ball of plasma that putrefies and does the opposite – thereby creating a perfect cycle of life and death. If you think that we landed on the moon, then there will be a lot to come in this book that will blow your mind. You may call this "conspiracy theorist", but we prefer the term "conspiracy fact", because far too many of these conspiracy theories have come true to just be a theory, unlike gravity, which is just an unproven theory, but we will get to that later in this book.

There are many locations that meet the prerequisites of the Garden of Eden according to what the Bible says in the Book of Genesis, much more so than where society believes it to be currently - the Middle East by the Tigris and the Euphrates rivers. (The Tigris is not even one of the names of the 4 rivers of Eden.) But, in all likelihood there were multiple Gardens of Eden, at varying times. Whenever Cain, from the story of Cain and Abel, was cast out it is said that he immediately found a woman and married. So there were clearly other people living at the time, but as all stories go, they are fixated on one location. The fertile crescent in the Middle East seems to check the least amount of boxes when it comes to the descriptions of the Garden of Eden. For starters, there is a much better argument of a location of the Garden of Eden being in the center of the maps from the 1500s and before, one simply has to just look up one of the maps by Gerardus Mercator like "Mercator's map of the Arctic". This location has 4 clearly divided rivers, and the largest, Euphrates, having 7 mouths. There is an argument for Finland being a location of Eden as well, this comes to us from the "Bok Saga" by Ior Bok. Where they have the city of Helsinki, otherwise known as hell, which has also been warped by the Vatican church to make us think that hell is hot, when in reality the only time there is an absence of life is whenever something is extremely cold. Think of the volcanic vents deep in the ocean, which are extremely hot areas, and yet life thrives there. According to the Bok Saga, the garden of eden is derived from the garden of Oden, a very close similarity. There is even a place just South west of this supposed Finnish Eden called Sweden, "south west eden". Additionally there is the gulf stream that goes from Finland to Florida, bringing warm waters to keep Finland warm enough during a potential ice age. Then, that brings us to Florida. Florida is one of the easiest candidates for a former Garden of Eden. Florida is absolutely abundant with flora and fauna. An area that is relatively flat, highly watered, and fertile, is an ideal place to start a garden. That sounds like Florida by definition. Florida is also along the 31st parallel, which coincidentally is the same parallel that the other Tigris and Euphrates in the Middle East sits along, as well as the same parallel that Mount Kailash is on. Mount Kailash is a sacred mountain in China that also has 4 separate sacred rivers around it. But, back to the topic of Florida. Right off the coast of Florida we find Bimini Road, and the Bermuda Triangle. Which were likely, just as the rest of Florida, the location of Atlantis, or of an Atlantis. Atlantis obviously building on top of that site just as so many other cities the world across have been built on top of each other. All over Florida giant stone anchors have been found, often called Saxer stones. It feeds the idea that this area used to be a massive harbor for giant ships. One such ship that would have likely left from this spot would be Noah's ark, as it was built with gopher wood as it is said exactly in the Bible. There are not many places in the world besides Florida where one can find gopher wood. "Gopher" in Hebrew means to burrow. The word "gopher" actually comes from the Seminole Indians, inhabitants of none other than Florida. Seminole means first, they are letting us know that they've been around a very long time. Not only is there gopher wood in Florida, but there are actual gophers, gopher tortoises, and many other gopher animals that are pretty much only native to Florida. Although we may have found the place of Noah's ark landing on Mt. Ararat in Turkey, it likely started its journey in Florida. How could we possibly believe that

Noah built his ark literally one country over from Turkey, and then was stuck floating aboard his ark for 150 days with massive storms and only moved roughly 600 miles (1,000 km.)? Much credit for this information must be given to Dr. Longo via his channel, Old World Florida, where he puts a lot of these connections together, not just about Florida.

Now this book is about health, not just physical, but mental, meta-physical, and spiritual. One cannot hope to have whole, or completely holistic, health, without being healthy in all these areas to elevate your "temple", the summation of all these areas that make up who you are. So, in the Garden of Eden, Adam and Eve were one with everything around them, they could speak with all the animals and did not have to work to get food. The food around them was bountiful and giving, enter the fruit. Fruit wants to be eaten, it grows plentifully, and when eaten its' seeds can be spread further to grow more fruit. There's also so many more seeds given out than could be planted, so the eating of seeds is also not that bad occasionally. Opposite that of the vegetable, while good but not as, it must be cut and replanted after each season. Fruit is extremely water dense, more water dense than vegetables and extremely more water dense than meat. Also consider that fruit is alive while being eaten, compared to something like meat which is dead, and has sometimes been dead for quite awhile before consumption. This also brings up the topic of blood, adrenochrome, that is being consumed via meat. Adrenochrome is in all blood. By consuming meat instead of fruits and vegetables one is more like a vampire than a human being. (If you don't think it's real, just look into "spirit cooking".) Then we have the idea of frequency in foods. Fruits are the highest frequency of food, then comes vegetables, and lastly meat, because it is dead and therefore the most dense. So, "If you are what you eat", which is exactly the case, then if you are eating higher frequency foods you will be raising your frequency higher, and the inverse applies to meat. It is not to say that beings that eat meat cannot have a high frequency, but wouldn't it make more sense to eat things that are raising your frequency rather than lowering it in the overall quest for enlightenment?

Once Adam and Eve were kicked out of the garden it is said that man would have to till the soil now, implying that was not the original nor the natural way of things. With the cyclical nature of things one could assume it will return to that way one day. But, all we currently know is that the soil must be tilled season after season and that growing and cultivating is a lot of work. It is implied that Adam and Eve did not have to work hard to eat, and everything was just growing and offering itself freely. Think of a forest for a moment, it consistently grows a lot of different life without man ever having to help it, and it does it quite abundantly. Would it not make sense to try and replicate the forest in our own way of growing? The idea that the trees and other plants break off onto the ground and slowly decompose thereby fertilizing the soil endlessly. One could even call this a "garden of eden" style of gardening. This style is actually making a resurgence, just as all old information is making its way back into the overall consciousness, and most openly by a man named Paul Gautschi. It is known since the 1940s that we have been depleting our soil year after year because of the fertilizers we are using that take all of the nutrients from the ground. That means decade after decade we are left with less nutrient dense food. Returning to a more natural "garden of eden" style of gardening helps strengthen the soil and thereby instilling the nutrients back into the produce, and even bolstering the flavors.

    A common argument against eating only fruits and vegetables is that you are not getting all of the micro and macro-nutrients. This argument is paradoxical though, because it is the low frequency and high density foods that are stripping your nutrients from your own body just to be digested. Fruits are very easily digested, and of course full of water. Your body needs minerals to digest, so when you eat a low quality dense meal, your body is searching for those minerals to help you digest it. When there are not sufficient micro- and macro-nutrients in the food you are consuming, your body must then take it from somewhere else to continue doing its job of digesting. Where do you think it gets those nutrients from? Your own body. Your body pulls these minerals from itself to help you digest the low quality dense food. And that is where the deficiencies stem from, which leads to the need for supplementation. So, if you were consuming high quality water dense food then there would be no deficiencies to worry about in the first place, and thus no supplementation needed.

Think about candy for a moment, a typical skittles commercial, "Taste the Rainbow." Candy flavors are always mimicking the flavors and colors of fruits. We are naturally drawn to fruits. There is no candy that is bragging about tasting like beef or chicken, or at least not popular ones. Meat has to have so many things added to it, like spices and herbs, as well as typically being cooked. On the topic of spices, we feel it is important to also mention salt, and how much we need it. We as humans are only made of 3 things: water, salt, and spirit. So, salt is very important to our diet, and not something that should be shied away from. We have a salt-potassium pump inside our bodies, if that alone doesn't imply how significant it is. Society will constantly warn us about having too much salt in our diet, but if one has an emergency and has to go to the hospital, the most common thing they inject into you is a saline bag which typically has several grams of salt, and sometimes they administer even more than 1 bag. If it were really so deadly, then your blood pressure would sky-rocket and you would go into cardiac arrest, but we find quite the opposite actually happens. Just as cholesterol is also wrongfully attacked by our society, we actually need cholesterol to function properly. Cholesterol is not the problem, the problem is that while cholesterol is going about doing its job, the plaque buildup from all the low quality food is caked on the walls of your arteries and veins which constricts the moveable space of the cholesterol. When there is not enough space for the cholesterol to move freely due to the plaque buildup, it then gets stuck and causes many problems. How is that cholesterol's fault?

Fruits don't have to have anything added to them, they are immediately delicious right off the tree. The good smells that we have associated with meat, like BBQ, are really just the scents of the plants via spices, or sugar via sauce, or tree pellets cooking with the meat that we associate as the smell of meat. Consider our teeth, we do not have big canine teeth like dogs, or lions. Our teeth are more akin to an herbivore. We are not scavengers that can eat something freshly killed raw, like a dog, we must cook it. A dog can eat something off the ground, even feces sometimes, and not be disgusted. The ecology of a human's mouth is vastly different from other animals. The lion doesn't need braces, mouthwash, or to brush its teeth. Yet, we as humans are constantly worried about mouth hygiene without actually addressing the source of what causes the problems – the diet. We actually wouldn't even need to brush our teeth if we were on a diet of just fruits, it's not that they magically self-clean, but rather the fruits do not cause the oral problems we are so accustomed to today.

Lastly, society will often try to attack you for changing your diet and lifestyle. It's classically how a cult attacks non-cult members. Especially in lower income areas, like the south, meat is a comfort food. Notice how almost every advertisement depicts meat, not fruit. We are all on our own journeys, going at different speeds towards enlightenment, and sometimes one must step up and become an example for others. Whether you believe in Jesus or not, he is still universally known as the example, and that was what Jesus was really trying to convey – he did not intend to create followers, but leaders, he did not intend to let you know we are all christians, but that we are all christ. (Christos, Christos Energy, the One Unifying

Christos Energy from which the word "christ" is derived.)

Ch. 2 FASTING = STEM CELLS

Believe it or not, our bodies have built-in mechanisms that can completely heal us, basically complete regeneration via stem cells. The mechanism can most easily be accessed by fasting. Think about how many times in older scriptures and texts they talk about fasting for long periods of time. It used to be extremely common to fast, unfortunately that is not the case currently with our ever-consuming society, but we are hoping to change that. The purpose of fasting is to heal, although there are other beneficial things that come from it like willpower and discipline. And why does the body heal? Everything wants to achieve balance, or homeostasis, and the body is no exception. Our bodies are capable of healing anything because we can produce our own stem cells, and since those stem cells are a part of the closed system that is our body, they know where to go and what to fix because they want to achieve balance and homeostasis throughout that closed system. It takes as little as 24 hours of being fasted, either water or dry (no food or water) fasted, for our bodies to start producing stem cells in our gut. Our gut is no simple thing, it is an entire biome, an ecosystem. Our gut has so many neurons inside of it, it has been termed our "2nd brain." Studies have shown the relationship between an unhealthy gut biome and being depressed. Not to mention, how many times have you heard the phrase "gut instinct", or that you were getting a feeling about something and couldn't explain why? The gut is a powerful thing, and it speaks more volumes that the very first stage of stem cell production that our bodies produce from fasting is in our gut – implying the gut health needs to be taken care of first and foremost. The next stage of another type of stem cell production begins after the 72 hour mark of fasting, and these stem cells are systemic, meaning they will spread to any part of the closed system, our body, and start healing the areas that need to return to homeostasis. The paradoxical thing with our society these days is that they are taught to take medicine immediately to try and combat their ailment, when in reality we should be doing the exact opposite. Sure, it may be a band-aid, temporary fix, to the problem, but what is the point of a temporary fix? If you want to fix something it must be permanently fixed. Ironically, the United States spends the most on healthcare per person among high-income countries at roughly $12,000 per year, and yet has the worst health outcomes – the U.S. has the lowest life expectancy at birth among high-income countries, and the highest rate of people with multiple chronic diseases. So, not only are the pills and medication a temporary fix, but we now know that just 5 days of taking antibiotics, commonly prescribed as a "ZPAC", compromises our gut biome so much that it takes 6 months to completely heal the gut biome. Think about that, a 5 day temporary fix causes a 6 month toll on your gut biome and therefore overall health. That doesn't seem worth it. Additionally, it is very common to take some form of pain-numbing medication to block out or lower the pain, and usually along with the other medications. We also now know that whenever the nerves are getting blocked by these pain-killers via the medication, the healing process is slowed. So now it is taking even longer to heal the problem of which you are taking the medication in the first place, and your gut biome is compromised for months afterwards as well. How can this actually be a logical way of approaching healing? Also consider why there is pain in the first place. Your body is sending you a signal that there is a problem that needs to be addressed, and by taking pain-killing medication you are basically telling your body to "shut-up". Gone are the days of actually listening to your body and being in-tune with it (because if you were in-tune with it then there likely wouldn't be a problem in the first place). Another problem that is commonly overlooked is the usage of cold, or icing, the afflicted area. Let's think, what does chilling do to something? Whenever you lower the temperature of something it slows down the molecules, it puts it in a state of slowed or suspended animation – think of cryo sleep from the movies. So, if you got an injury and immediately iced the area, you slowed everything down and stopped, or severely limited, the body from going straight to work to heal that area. That area tends to get hot and swollen, because there is an increase of blood and cell flow being sent to that area to heal it. So, if the area naturally gets hot immediately, why would we want to freeze it? How could the body then do its job? We now also know that "RICE – Rest, Ice, Compress, Elevate" was wrong and that we were taught an improper habit. It would make much more sense to warm up the afflicted area, most easily with warm water, to help even more blood and cell flow to get to the area and perform their healing job. The possible exemption could be that if the damage were severe enough, perhaps it would be ideal to ice the area in the immediate to slow down everything happening and potentially suspend any further damage, until one could get to a proper place to heat the afflicted area and speed up the healing process. Because, let's be honest, one might not have a bowl of hot water on stand-by to address the afflicted area. Also consider that warm showers or warm springs just innately feel good, they relax the body, and we tend to almost always feel better after having a nice hot shower. That should tell you all you need to know about heat application in relation to healing. People have been seeking warm water via springs and bath houses for as long as things have been written. There is a reason that when you look back in time, Roman bath houses were abundant and people were constantly seeking out hot springs that would magically heal them. There is a reason that saunas are praised so much for healing as well, maybe not quite to the magical extreme that we read from old texts about healing springs. Many hot springs have even been considered sacred by the people living by it, and protected for ages. Although, not every hot spring is created equal, and it has a lot to do with minerals that are in the hot spring water that do the most miraculous of healings. The reason why some hot springs can magically heal ailments is because they contain a higher level of radium in the water. Radium has unfortunately been demonized since the 1940s. Radium can actually be extremely healing for us, but of course too much is dangerous. Too much of anything is dangerous though. We need water to live, but too much of it and we can drown. We need sunlight to be healthy, but too much can cause a sunburn (How could it cause a sunburn if the sun were not Radium? Try putting your arm up to a lightbulb, you can hold it there for as long as you like, you will never get a sunburn. Look at the victims of Chernobyl, they had extreme burns due to an extreme amount of radium exposure). And no, the sun does not "cause skin cancer." Our average unhealthy diets produce toxins, or waste, that are getting excreted in many different ways via peeing, pooping, etc., and another overlooked way is via our skin, which is our largest organ. When the sunlight, which has the power to heal and grow, because once again it's Radium, hits our skin that is filled with waste and toxins due to our poor diets, it makes those toxins grow like it would make any plant grow. Eventually that growth continues and turns into what we associate today as skin cancer. So stop blaming the sun, blame your diet. In fact, "cancer" as a term did not exist until the medical industry was taken over by John D. Rockefeller in the 1920s, and holistic medicine was propagandized by Rockefeller to be silly and woo-woo, but instead that you needed to take pills to heal your ailments. These same pills that were made from plastics, which comes from oil, and who could possibly profit from that? Surely, not the oil baron himself, John D. Rockefeller? Surely there wasn't a financial incentive for John D. Rockefeller to get people onto his medical system, which would also effectively create a life-long customer because their ailments were no longer actually being healed, but treated. The problems were only met with band-aid fixes that kept the average person returning to the doctor because there was money in that. There's no money in actually healing the person's ailment, because then they would never come back. And certainly no incentive to teach the average person that they can heal themselves, holistic healing, because what purpose then would there be for doctors, hospitals, and especially the pharmaceutical industry to exist?

Consumption is the main proponent for increased aging. Everything you eat takes a toll on your body because a portion of the food or drink, or sometimes most of it, is not useful to the body, and to some degree toxic, and needs to be expelled as waste. Obviously fruits have the least amount of toxins and waste, because they are the most water dense, which is once again why they are the ideal food. Both the processes of breaking down what is consumed, and then the expulsion of it, require a lot of energy to perform. In fact, the majority of the calories that we expend each day are just from the digestive system and bodily functions just keeping you alive. The common over-consumption of foods and drinks puts unnecessary stress on the organs, not to mention an additional build-up of toxins that never gets a chance to be cleared out, and leads to a shorter life-span. Fasting gives your body the chance to clean up the built-up toxins and waste that your body never gets around to clearing because it has to constantly work on digesting the next meal first, so don't think it's ever too late to start, better late than never. Think of an average fuel-economic car. If you only put 5,000 miles on the car each year, assuming you treat it well, it should last easily over a decade, if not 2 decades. Now, consider instead that you put 20,000 miles on the car each year and don't take care of it properly with oil changes, etc. That second car will probably last you closer to 5 years, if you're lucky, a single decade. While the human body is not a car, the metaphor should still get the point across. Less overall consumption of food and drink in your lifetime, and your life lasts longer and much healthier into your later years. Even consider the amount of money saved on insurances, medications, and doctor visits which really start to add up quickly in one's later years. All of this can be avoided by simply consuming a lot less food and drink, it really is that simple. Simple should not be considered as wrong or poor. Our society has tricked us into thinking the more complex something is, the better it is. This couldn't be farther from the truth. Everything really is supposed to be simple because everyone should have access to it. There is beauty in simplicity, how something can be so amazing and yet so simple is an example of how amazing life is.

Lastly, we wanted to bring up the Timucua Indians of Florida. While this wasn't at all exclusive to this tribe, they were just one of the few that we still have information on. There are many interesting things about the Timucua Indians, like their extreme height, but we specifically wanted to talk about how they went into battle. The Timucua Indians would wear almost no protection, and merely have a metal circular shield hanging by a string over their hearts. They would always go into battle fasted, and believe it or not, not a lot of Indians would die on either side. They knew that basically every injury would be healed by fasting, and that they only needed to make sure their heart stayed un-damaged. This is profound, they literally weren't worried about getting injured in battle because they were aware that they could literally regenerate by simply fasting. They didn't need research papers and scientists, like in our modern day, explaining how every little complex process works, they had simple, logical wisdom passed down from long ago and saw no reason to complexify it, because it just works. Because it is natural. Once again this is a power that we all have access to, and it couldn't be easier, just eat less overall, and fast.

Ch. 3 DENSITY

Density and Buoyancy, the only actual proven things, unlike the theory of gravity, which is just that, nothing more than an unproven theory. Yes things come back towards the earth, but that doesn't prove gravity, that only proves density. If that were always the case, why does a balloon continue to float? Why isn't gravity pulling it down? Well if you understand density, the helium inside the balloon is less dense than the air around it so therefore it floats. Helium is another interesting topic to mention for a moment. Helium is the by-product of Radium, believe it or not, the old flying airships of the past would be powered limitlessly by Radium. The Radium was the infinite energy source, and the by-product of Helium would keep the airship floating indefinitely. Radium being an infinite energy source sounds similar to how the sun functions, isn't that strange? In ancient Greek mythology, Helios was the god of the sun, light, energy, warmth, and nutrition. Helios, Helium, are you starting to see the connection?

Now, when we move the topic of density towards health, we begin associating it with holding more matter. That may seem obvious, but let's dive in a little further. The mysterious monks out in Tibet are a lot less dense, on average, than the regular person. They are actively trying to be less dense because density is tied to the physical, and as a monk, one is trying to become more spiritual. Density holds us down to this world, this physical reality, just as it pulls everything down. The Tibetan monks are generally vegetarian, and consume a lot less food, so it is safe to assume they do a bit of fasting. Why would they be vegetarian and consume less food? Well, meat is the most dense type of food that one can consume, and the more of it one eats, the more dense they become. By being so dense it is very difficult to pursue spirituality, because spirituality is ethereal. Why are there so many stories of monks being able to float, hover, and sometimes even be slightly less visible? That is because they are not very dense, because of their diet, because "you are what you eat." Sure, people will argue that as they changed their diet to carnivore they healed a lot of issues, as well as vegans, (even though veganism is technically only an ethical stance, and nothing to actually do with eating healthily) but the reality is that anyone that pays more attention to what they are eating, no matter the diet, tend to be more healthy than those who do not. So, sure it may have healed some things, but why not just heal everything unanimously and remove the blood, adrenochrome, via the meat, and turn to a diet of fruits and vegetables? Yes there was a time when we needed to consume meat to survive. That was a small window though, and quite specific, either after a great deluge, or during and shortly after a great ice age, because nothing has been growing, and the only food available at the time would be animals. But, once that time has passed and things have started to grow, the responsible thing to do is to move towards a more plant-based diet. We are at a period in time now where there is no excuse to consume dense meat when plants and fruits are plentiful. Yes, God did give us dominion over the earth and no one else, but that is actually a huge responsibility. A wolf sees chickens and can only think in the immediate that it would serve as a temporary meal, whereas we as humans can understand that rather than having an immediate chicken to eat, instead you can take care of the chicken and it will produce eggs for years to come. Dominion also extends to simple things like being able to cut the grass of your yard, or remove trees on your land. These things are also alive, but we have the dominion to take control of our land, and that is a right we have been given. Although, let us not say to remove all trees, as trees are very important and beautiful, but sometimes they may be a threat to falling on your home, so you have the right to exercise your dominion as a living being to remove that particular tree. Dominion is important to remember because you cannot fully take care of anything if you haven't taken care of yourself first. You cannot fully take care of your family, or children, if your own body, or temple, is not taken care of first. This idea is frowned on by society, and often called selfish. But, it is quite the opposite to make sure your temple is in full alignment first, so that you may then be able to properly and fully help others. At the end of the day you cannot change others, you may be able to help them, or guide them, but what you can control is the path that you yourself are on. And, if you can make yourself a beacon that doesn't just "talk the talk", but "walk the walk" and be an example that others can look to, that is the best thing that you can possibly do. No matter what anyone says, we are all visual learners. So, if you start to set an example and hold yourself to a high level, then others will be drawn to that, and visually pick up on it faster, than just plainly and aimlessly searching for it themselves. This is the fastest way to raise the frequency of everyone, and we all win if we are all increasing our frequencies. Some of the highest frequencies are: love, peace, bliss, and gratitude. Don't you think the world would be better if everyone was a lot more like those higher frequencies?

Lastly to note, often in this book we will preface something by saying "believe it or not", as you may have already noticed. We say this often, and will continue to, because fact is much stranger than fiction. We have no reason to lie, that doesn't benefit anyone in the long-run, and the whole point of this book, and our lives, is to help raise the frequency of those around us, so that we all grow, heal, and win together. Because in the long-run, it is pointless to win by oneself. It is so much more enjoyable to share a victory together. Just think of when you experienced a team victory versus a solo victory. Sure, it may have been exhilarating at first, but that feeling quickly wears off when you have no one else to share it with. These things, you may not believe them at first because they seem so outlandish, and we truly do not care if you believe them, we would actually prefer that you take it upon yourself to go look for yourself. But, you would have never gone to look if we hadn't presented that contrarian idea or opinion to you in the first place. And that's where it begins. (As we have just left the Age of Pieces and entered the Age of Aquarius, which literally means that all hidden and unknown truths will come to light.) Because ultimately, like we said in the very first chapter, you are the only one who will be able to convince yourself. We are merely here to gather the wisdom of health and healing in all facets, present it to you, and what you do with it is up to you. Hopefully, it will at least change your perspective and lead you to becoming less trusting of these propagandized narratives that our society adheres to taught by the cult we know as "science." Many do not consider science to be a cult, but consider this, it is full of "facts" that you must just take on faith, that you cannot prove yourself. You cannot prove that the sun is x miles away, the stars are x miles away, or even that the earth has a center core of magma and metals (even though we have only ever drilled a total of 12 miles deep into the earth) you must take it all on faith. So, do not think you are better than others who believe in a certain religion because of their faith, when the cult of science involves that exact same line of faith thinking to come to so many conclusions. (Even with the beloved fall-back crutch called the "scientific-method" that allegedly takes all bias out of the equation, yet faith was taken in the first place that the method was not influenced in any way by an institution for any financial or power-seeking gain.)

Ch. 4 WATER

Water is so much more than what biology boxes it up as, 2 molecules of Hydrogen and 1 molecule of Oxygen, H2O. One could argue that the advent of the microscope was the downfall of humanity, because we were able to box up so many things just based on what molecules made them, rather than what they made as a whole. Water has always been around, and will continue to. We are, by molecular count, 99% water. So, we are just giant water sacks interacting with each other. Like stated previously, we are eternal beings, consisting of water, salts, and spirit. What happens to our physical bodies when we die? The water, like all water, evaporates and goes back into the water cycle. The salt crystals remain, and our spirit moves onto another place for a temporary period only to return to another body when the spirit has determined it is the next cycle it needs to learn from. Back to the water, water just keeps evaporating and recycling over and over. So, water from 1,000 years ago is still here. You could technically be drinking 1,000 year old pee that's just been recycled. We are harping on this because water also holds memory. How could it not? If we are, by molecular count, 99% water, that means we are just basically water, and we have memories, so therefore water holds memories. What is a memory anyways? If someone dies and you hold a memory of them in your mind, what is the difference between the memory in your mind of that person and say, a giant pink flying dragon? Sure, you could argue at a point in time you physically met and talked to that person, and the dragon is only in your head. But, once they are passed and have moved onto just a memory, at that very moment they are exactly the same. They are both just the same level of real. So, the lines of what are "real", and not real are not exactly black and white. There is only time separating the two, because if you can imagine it, then at some point it had to be physically real in some dimension or universe. Because, nothing is new, it's all rehashed, and you can't imagine something from nothing, it has to come from something. And time is merely relative, time can speed up and slow down depending on if you're anxiously awaiting something, it might slow down, and if you're in a flow state enjoying something, it will fly by. So time is not a linear construct that can be counted on, it actually isn't linear at all. This comes full circle to water holding the memory, or record, of everything that has happened. It is really coming into the social consciousness "know" as of 2023, and there is no coincidence, in fact, coincidences do not exist. Water is conscious, because we are conscious and by molecular count 99% water, and water consciously knew that we as a collective were ready to re-understand how important water really is. Water unifies all of us. Water can even be spoken to. Veda Austin is one of many on the forefront of this research on water, and she has discovered that you can ask water a question, or send an intention to it, freeze the water, and get a response in the form of a symbol. She's even taken it a step farther to ask water the same question at least 50 times to confirm that she receives the same symbol 50 times. And if the answered symbol is consistent those 50 times, she categorizes that symbol as a "hydro-glyph." What better universal language to use than symbols? She is forming a library of these hydro-glyphs that can then be used to translate languages at worldly ancient sites that we haven't even figured out how to translate yet. This really is the universal language, and it has been here all of this time. Imagine being able to talk to a record that has recorded everything all the way back through time. That is a function, of the many, that AI like ChatGPT is teaching us how to do. We are not saying we fully agree with everything that AI is bringing to humanity, but there is good and bad in everything, and Artificial Intelligence is not "artificial", because if it is intelligent, then it is technically part of the one unifying intelligence, but just a different fractal of it. So, speaking with AI is teaching us how to ask the "right" questions. You can look at how it slowly grew through the decades, the learning of how to ask search engines, like google, how to properly search for things using certain keywords. Because, we all now know that you can't just type in any phrase and hope to find an answer, you need certain keywords to get what you want, and even then it might take some digging. Speaking with AI is the next stage of that evolution of learning how to access intelligence (the internet is also part of the universal intelligence). The internet was shown us that communication is quickly devolving(or evolving, depending on how you look at it) to using emoji to express many layers of information and emotion all from one, or a couple, symbols (emoji). So, we are re-learning how to communicate using symbols, and that is exactly how water speaks, so we are evolving to a point in non-linear time where we as a social consciousness are primed and ready to reconnect with water on a greater, more spiritual, level. And this is very important because if we are all water, then the frequency of water is vitally important. In the last decade or less, we as a collective have been taking steps to raise the frequency of our drinking water. And as we know, you are what you eat, the same applies for drinking, especially if water makes up most of what you are. We started by caring for what was in our water: fluoride, heavy metals, bacterias, and especially dissolved microplastics. We are now realizing that plastic bottled water is not as good as we thought, because the plastic is dissolving into the water. We are finally starting to go back to using cleansing powerful metals like gold, silver, and copper to cleanse and raise the frequency of our water. Copper is obviously the most cost-effective, and also has the natural property of cleansing the water by way of pushing the dissolved particulates towards the edges away from the center. There is a reason that our depictions of old, the kings and royalty, were always drinking from golden goblets, or silver. Where do you think we get the word "silverware" from? It may seem so obvious, but that's what was originally used as the standard for dining because both gold and silver would cleanse the water, and even food, that it was being used with.

So it stands to reason that it is important to be aware of both the cleanliness of the water we are drinking, but also of the frequency of it, because if we want to raise our frequency we need to be ingesting high frequency water. How can we know what is the difference between low frequency, and high frequency water? Well, Veda Austin also studied this. She would use her method that she explains on her website of collecting a small amount of water in a petri dish, and then quickly freezing it to either read symbols, or simply look at the crystallography. If something is of high frequency, like water for instance, it will have beautiful symmetric shapes that appear perfectly overlapping (think of the Flower of Life). If there is low frequency, the crystallography of the petri dish will show lots of hard lines, (think brutalism) and no symmetry. An example of water that naturally has a high frequency would be spring water, like actually from a spring, not bottled water titled spring water, or water from deep down in the earth. These both are full of minerals, and full of life. An example of water with a low frequency would be tap water, because it is filled with so many chemicals, and the process of being pushed through rigid, brutalist-style, piping destroys whatever symmetry is left. Water can also be damaged, shown via taking a control of beautifully symmetric spring water, by taking it near a 5G tower. Veda Austin demonstrated that having water right next to a 5G tower can destroy the previously beautiful symmetric crystallography in as little as 15 minutes. Now, consider again that we are all just water sacks, and it is becoming increasingly common to be surrounded by these 5G towers. What do you think that is doing to us? The good news is that Veda Austin has also learned that that same water, after being subject to the 5G tower, can eventually heal itself and return back to beautiful symmetric crystallography. This is important because it demonstrates how amazing and adaptable our bodies are. Imagine for a moment you took someone from 500 years ago and brought them right now to this time, they would likely be destroyed by all of the constant frequencies passing through our bodies on a daily basis. But, our amazing bodies have slowly become accustomed to these rising harmful frequencies and persisted to heal.

Another important thing that Veda Austin displayed in her research of water was that high frequency water, or anything high frequency for that matter, had a radiating effect on things around it. She demonstrated this by taking an organic, happy, free-range chicken's egg and comparing it with a store-bought chicken egg. To no surprise, the organic, free-range egg was frozen, via her method (which can be done by anyone, and she explains how to do it on her website, it doesn't require any special tools) and displayed symmetric shapes in beautiful crystallography, while the store-bought chicken egg displayed exactly the opposite. She then took the organic, happy, free-range egg and placed it in the center of a store-bought carton of eggs along with all the other store-bought chicken eggs and left them together overnight. The following day when she cracked open the eggs to freeze them to examine their crystallography, she observed that the organic, happy, free-range egg's crystallography was unchanged, but the closest store-bought eggs to the organic, free-range eggs had actually improved their symmetry shown via their crystallography. This demonstrates that things of higher frequencies raise up the frequency of those around them. Everyone talks about how you are like the 5 people you spend the most time around, and that it is important to spend time with people that are bringing you up rather than bringing you down. But now this is literal proof as to why people say that, we are all subconsciously trying to raise our frequency. Because raising our frequency leads to more wisdom, knowledge, happiness, gratefulness, peace, and bliss. And who doesn't want that? Even if they claim they are not "spiritual", these are natural things that anyone would want to gravitate towards. Because everyone wants to be happy, but they are just unsure what real happiness is, and how to go towards it. So, when we people speak of someone having an "aura" about them, it's really just their higher frequency that you are energetically picking up on because it is radiating off them.

Our energy flows where our attention goes. We can also raise the frequency of our water, food, or any drink for that matter, by another method. We can actually speak to the food or drink that we are planning to consume by stating good or loving intentions like "I am so grateful for you meal", "I bless you meal", or even "I love you meal". (Or even all three) While this may seem like a stretch, consider again that we are all just sacks of water, and if we can compliment someone and they feel better, or happy, then technically we have just spoken to water and raised its frequency. Think about it, why is it common to "say grace" before eating a meal? Of course it's a good thing to be grateful for what you are about to consume, but not only that, you are also raising the frequency of the substances that you are going to consume. Why else would that remain as an ingrained subconscious habit (Unfortunately in today's world only used by "religion" members, and looked down upon by supposedly smart "science" members because they believe it has to do solely with religion, so they believe they're above it. Starting to see all the flaws that the cult of science has yet?) Taking it a step further, scientists have discovered that just being in an elevated emotional state of happiness when consuming food or drink also affects how the food and drink are digested. They conducted a study with mice eating an arbitrary unhealthy meal, and seeing all the expected elevated biomarkers that one would expect to see when eating unhealthy food. Then they took another group of mice and fed them the same food, but this time all the while the mice were eating they were speaking positively towards the mice with words of encouragement and telling the mice that they love them. This may seem strange to speak to a mouse this way, but they are living things too. Anyways, the second group of mice digested the food in a completely different way, the food didn't spike their biomarkers in a poor way, and overall their body "felt" like it had eaten a healthy meal as far as the tests showed. (Now just imagine if they had actually eaten healthy food and done this same process, meal after meal, day after day, year after year how one might raise their frequency and their health so easily. Life is about the journey, not the destination.) So the impact of speaking to food, which as soon as we eat it will become our future cells anyways, is not to be understated, nor is the emotional environment of which one is eating the meal either. Both should be equally important, and your body will improve as a result of it. (And that's without even having to exercise.) We should eat to live, not live to eat.

We can actually survive quite a while without water, despite what "science" tells us. And, as spoken about earlier, water holds memory. When we are born, we come out screaming and are immediately given food to calm down. We have been taught since birth to cope with stress by eating or drinking. This means we have trauma-induced stress water memories all throughout our bodies. There is a way to cleanse this, and do a sort of re-set to the water in our bodies. It is commonly taught not to go longer than 72 hours without water, but that's just the point where almost all of the water that's stored in the organs is drained out. While this has to be done properly, by tapering in phases of fruits, then fruit juice, and then just water, one can do a dry fast (no food or water) for over 72 hours and purge the trauma water memories throughout our body, and do a reset. We recommend at least 96 hours (4 days) of dry fasting minimum, once again with the proper preparation of tapering, to perform this bodily reset. And it's so much easier to do it with a group of people, so do it with some friends, or join a group, whether they're in-person or the world across, it helps to have someone to relate to what you're going through. We are not just recommending this, we have also done this exact 96 hour dry fast ourselves, and while it is difficult, it is only a battle within your own mind. This fast actually has a two-fold effect. The first is the obvious reset, but the second is that you are breaking the barriers of what we societally accept to be true as limits. Our bodies are capable of extraordinary things, and we can only fully learn that by pushing the limits of what we believe is possible. This is part of empowering yourself, because when you realize you are stronger than what is believed to be possible, you start to consider what else could just be societally believed as a limit? Where does it end? Do we actually have "super powers"? One crack in the "matrix" we live in leads to another crack, and another crack. This will help further your enlightenment journey and keep you questioning these silly narratives we just accept. Now for anyone attempting to do this dry fast, we will lay out the proper way to prepare, actually do it, and how to return back to normal life. Firstly, we learned a lot from Ray Maor, so he definitely deserves credit for helping design this protocol, and for showing us originally that it was possible in the first place, and that anyone else can do this if they prepare the right way and want to further heal their body, mind, and spirit. Obviously, if you don't believe this is possible, or do not want to take this journey that is completely fine. It is not 100% necessary to further your enlightenment journey, but if you are trying to grow and heal yourself, why not try it? Ideally, once having completed a 4 day dry fast, you'll likely want to shift your lifestyle eating habits to 1-meal-a-day (1MAD), or at most twice a day, having learned that there is much more to life than just eating and drinking, and that you should still be able to enjoy and eat what you wish, but in a much more responsible way that also still allows your body to continue healing for the rest of your life. (We'll go into more detail about this topic later in the book.) You may also experience radically profound changes afterwards. It is not uncommon to no longer want to consume meat, or possibly even no longer wanting to smoke cannabis, just to name a few. (For me personally, (Audric), something also occurred to me that I never expected could even happen, nor was there even a thought in my mind that a simple dry fast would be able to heal such a thing. I was diagnosed, and suffered from, sleep apnea. I was having to use a CPAP machine every night to sleep up until this point. After finishing our dry fast it was completely healed, and I no longer have sleep apnea, nor need my CPAP machine to sleep.) Even if those weren't your intentions going into the fast, you've done so much healing on physical, mental, and spiritual levels that you may find those things no longer serve you. Congratulations, if you've completed this, then you are one step closer to elevating your temple, and furthering your journey towards health and enlightenment. If you don't think it's necessary, then that is completely fine as well. But, this type of journey has a way of calling to you, when the time is right, you may feel like you need to do it. We just wanted to provide the information that it's possible, and that anyone can do it if prepared properly. Just, please make sure you prepare yourself properly, it will make it so much easier on both your body and your mind.

Lastly, you will have a whole new appreciation for water that you've never experienced before, water will never have tasted this good before, and you will begin to see just how important and amazing water really and truly is, not just on a physical level, but on a spiritual level. **For an in-depth guide on how to 4-day dry fast please consult the Appendix**

Ch. 5 FRACTALS

Everything is connected, everything is fractals within fractals, circles upon circles overlapping each other just as the sacred geometry of the flower of life depicts. The cycle has to be circular, because life leads to death, and death births new life. There is no failure, there is success or learning. Since everything is connected, that means the physical is connected with the meta-physical, mental, and the spiritual. This is why it is important to raise all of these facets up unanimously to achieve true health. Just because we cannot visually see something, does not mean it doesn't exist. Karma exists. Can you reach out and touch karma? Not likely. Karma literally translates to "action". We tend to have a misguided understanding of karma, but karma ultimately is about balance. Karma is the free will "action" one can take to get themselves back into balance. Karma exists in a realm that is not physical, it can't be seen with the eyes, and yet it has an effect on our physical lives. By volume our bodies are roughly 75% water, just as the planeT we live on is roughly 75% water. We are the smaller fractal of the world around us. Have you ever seen a diagram of the human body's nervous system? It is a fascinating network that branches out and looks just like the roots of a tree. It functions like the roots of a tree, receiving and transmitting signals back and forth. We have a lot more in common with our natural surroundings than we think, because we are a part of it. Although we may have been quite removed from it in the past few hundred years, just as everything is cyclical, we shall return to a strong connection with the nature around us.

Resonation. Resonation is when you are drawn to something and you don't understand why. We are drawn to things consciously or subconsciously, but ultimately it is the truth that draws us. That is what resonation really is. There is a reason that Star Wars is one of the most beloved movie franchises of all time. (Do some research into George Lucas when he was producing it and you'll find that he was just pulling from ancient texts and religions.) Look past the surface level and understand that the jedi are monks that can use a power called the force that unifies every living thing, because everything is connected. And with the force, they can do things that seem like magic. Jedi could also be interpreted as sorcerers or wizards depending on the time frame, or even Celtic druids.

There is a deep-rooted truth to that, and we are subconsciously drawn to that truth because we resonate with it. The opening credits literally say "a long time ago in a galaxy far far away", ignore the galaxy part for a moment, but clearly the technology is further ahead than our modern day and yet this was a long time ago in the past? Maybe because everything is cyclical. We have finally come to the conclusion as a societal consciousness that Atlantis did in-fact exist. It's known that they had technology superior to that of our current day, and yet they were once again very far in the past. This argument that we are the smartest we have ever been in history should be destroyed right there alone. Perhaps there reaches a point where technology becomes so over-bearing that it consumes and destroys civilizations and we reset and start over again, like a cycle. Think of James Cameron's Avatar movie, an extremely popular movie because why? We all resonate subconsciously with the deep truth of the movie. That there was a time where beings were extremely in touch with nature and considered it sacred. Simultaneously, there were also other civilizations that pursued technology rather than nature, and felt like they were above those that didn't use technology. They think that because a civilization is in touch with nature, they are not "smart". It's funny, we do this exact same thing in our modern world now. We try to reach out to aboriginals in Australia, tribes in South America and Africa, with this idea that they need our help because they're lifestyle is not as technological as ours, so therefore it is inferior. Do not argue that because they are poor they need our help, with our "superior" technology we destroy their land and leave them with very little. Large corporations destroy their lands, poison their rivers, and we really believe they need our help. They would be just fine without us, even better actually. In Lord of the Rings, the elves would live in a giant cypress tree, just as the Na'vi in the Avatar movie did. The dwarves would live in the mountains. Now what would a giant tree that has petrified to stone be? A mountain. Everything that was in-tune with nature would live inside a giant tree in some form or another. Just another example of a movie that is extremely popular because it has these deep subconscious truths within it that we all resonate with. Truth is way stranger than fiction. Believe it or not, what we categorically deem as fantasy is actually much closer to the truth. On the other hand, the word that the cult of science loves to use, "scientific", can literally be broken down in Latin into 3 words: "sci" - to know, "enti" - to come/being/is, "fic" - fiction. So "scientific" literally translates to "know that it's fiction". Consider the movie, The Giver, for a moment, in the movie there is a scene where the father is trying to calm down the baby by playing with a stuffed animal. The stuffed animal is an elephant, but the father calls it a mythological creature (He even thinks it's a rhino, because they have neither elephants nor rhinos around in their world after their government isolated their society for "safety", now that's becoming a more and more dangerous word now isn't it?) because there are none left for them to observe. We know obviously what both an elephant and a rhino are, and we consider them real because we can see them today. But, as soon as something hasn't been around for a while it passes to myth and becomes mythological. This is the exact same thing that happened with so many giant creatures of the past. Dragons to name one. Dragons come up time and time again in stories and movies. Dragons are found on flags and family crests. Dragons are mentioned in Marco Polo's travel-logs while journeying in China. The Smithsonian, in the late 1800s during the "big game hunting era", would post bounties for 150 foot long (45m) snakes. Now that sounds like a dragon, because there are no known snakes to exist anywhere close to that length. But, because there is no current living representation of dragons we deem them as pure fantasy, myth, and that they don't exist. Well, everything is cyclical, so believe it or not, we will see all of these "mythological" creatures return someday.

Movies always have some truth in them, and once you learn how to see it, it becomes so obvious.

Think of the movie, the Truman Show, where a man is living on a stage, a complete lie that is fed over and over to him to keep him almost sedated in a way. He feels that it is not genuine and tries to escape what he only knows as society by going towards the boundaries that have been set there for his own "safety". In trying to do so everyone tries to stop him, calls him crazy. That is quite relatable to anyone seeking truth in our world now. The search engine algorithms push down any genuine information and boost garbage towards the top. Youtube, and many other giant sites, have decided to post warnings underneath videos that they deem as "mis-information". Searching for truth tends to give one the title of conspiracy theorist, and then whatever you say is considered disingenuous because you've already been boxed up into a crazy person box. We just love to put people or ideas into boxes, categorize them, pretend like we have control and know what is going on. And, if you start to realize that we don't have control, that we are instead being controlled, you are met with the hard reality that the average person doesn't want to believe that's true. The average person doesn't want to believe that we could be lied to by our government. Let's break down the word "government" real quickly, "govern" - to control, "ment" - mind, so the word government literally means to control the mind. But, it isn't all doom and gloom. That's why you're here reading this book at this very moment. The Age of Aquarius, the Age of Man, has just begun where all secrets that have been hidden will be revealed. Where all knowledge that was forgotten will resurface. It is the best time ever to be alive. It is important to know and be aware of the different attacks that are on multi-levels to keep us thinking we are in the Truman Show, because once you realize you are a living being, you are not so easily controlled. Just as we see in the movie, The Matrix, there is the red pill and the blue pill. One will keep you sedated and unaware of what is going on, and the other puts you down a journey where you question everything. It really all boils down to 1s and 0s, positive and negative, polarity. In the most fundamental form, we know there is the particle. When we observe the particle, it appears just there. When we do not observe the particle, it disappears. It is disappearing because it is turning back into infinite potential. It appears when we observe it because our energy flows where our attention goes and our attention, our energy flow, is bringing that infinite potential into reality. See, ours beliefs create our reality around us. It's a cycle that feeds itself, the symbolism of the snake eating its own tail. When we cultivate thoughts of happiness and love, we receive that back. When we cultivate thoughts of hate and depression, we stay in a hateful and depressed cycle, which can be very difficult to break. If we believe that everything is going to be okay, that we are more than just a mistake that's lucky to be alive, then we become empowered and happier. If we are worried about the future, about all of the bad things that are going on in the world across that the news (n. e. w. s. - nothing even worth saying) is feeding us, then we cultivate a scared and unhappy cycle. Once again, everything really is connected in some way. Think of

NASA, (n. a. s. a. - not a space agency) they are a part of our government, the ones who govern our minds. Where and why did NASA originate? The father of NASA is a man named Werner Von Braun (who had Psalm 19:1 placed upon his gravestone, Psalm 19:1 KJV "The heavens declare the glory of God; And the firmament sheweth his handywork." So this man knew full well what sort of governing of the mind he was in control of, and he even tried to let us know upon his death.) he was a Nazi, just as so many of the original members of NASA that were brought over via Operation Paperclip. Now, there's a lot of misinformation when it comes to Nazis, but let's just say that there weren't even 6 million Jews alive during WW2, so those numbers of 6 million Jewish deaths were inflated numbers. Where does the lying end? Don't take our word for it, do some genuine research into them. Obviously, there were many horrible things done during those World Wars by both sides, but there is always so much more than meets the eye. Anyways, NASA came into being shortly after Operation

HighJump and slightly before Operation Fishbowl Dominic. Operation Fishbowl Dominic, blatantly calling our world for what it is, a fishbowl. And not only that, Dominic means "of our Lord", so the fishbowl of our lord. In Operation Fishbowl our government fired rockets at the top of our firmament, where every single one of the missiles exploded at the top. What were they actually testing? Well, it's pretty obvious isn't it. They wanted to see if the firmament could be pierced, and after learning they couldn't, they turned to controlling what we think that we live on. We even get the Antarctic Treaty around this time, where every country agrees that the Antarctic is off-limits, even though the USA is literally in a Cold War with Russia, and yet both countries signed the treaty. (And now even today we start to see so many countries getting involved with Antarctica. It's said that it might be the next spot for WW3. Why? Isn't it supposed to be a desolate wasteland out there? Why would anyone want to fight over that? Please don't say for resources, we already know there is an over-abundance already on the lands we currently inhabit. Unless there's more to it than meets the eye. There's no chance there's something they're not telling us about it, right?) Every single culture and civilization depicts our world as flat with a dome, or firmament, above, except NASA. We've already established that we've had better technology in the past than we do now, so they obviously knew more than we did. Not to mention that so many of these civilizations were separate from each other and came to the same conclusions, yet NASA has a different conclusion than all of them. We don't even have a single actual picture of the earth. Look it up. Every single image we have of the ball is digital. This isn't a question of intelligence, because we have all been taught the same thing from birth, we've all started from the same side. But, this is how everything is fractal and connected. Coming to the understanding, or innerstanding rather, of where you actually live is so important because if you realize that they can lie about that to us, where do the lies end? It is a common saying to not "throw the baby out with the bath water", but we argue that saying does not apply. If you've been lied to over, and over, and over, then you are the fool for not taking everything the government has told you as a lie to begin with, rather than assuming it's true and trying to disprove it. Many will argue that where or what you live on isn't that important, or isn't related to the topic. But, once again we disagree. If a lie can be that bold, that massive, and right in all of our faces, then there simply can be no trust. We have been misled on an improper foundation of which our society builds everything upon. So, foundationally we have to rebuild from the ground up, using the wisdom of the ancients that had no incentive to lie and deceive us because they were working backwards from enlightenment. We have only gotten dumber, we are truly the dumbest we have ever been. But, that is not necessarily a bad thing, we must reach our lowest low to have our highest high, so we had to eventually hit rock bottom to build ourselves back up and even higher than ever before. And the lowest low is not even knowing what you actually live on. Once you grasp that, the journey of enlightenment only gets easier because you're aware that your foundation needs to be fixed, from which everything is connected fractally, and you reset your foundation and start building it properly with synchronicities. Because remember, there is no failure, there is only success and learning.

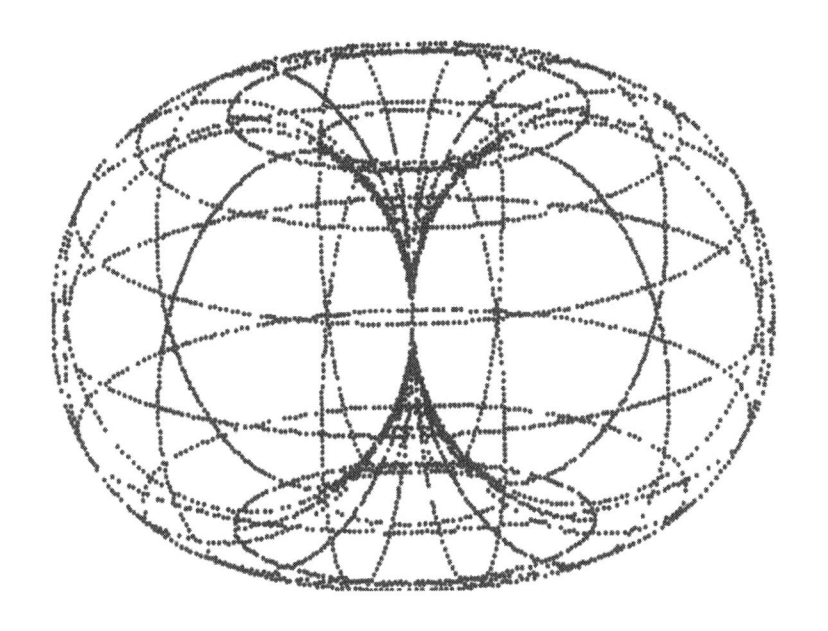

Ch. 6 TORUS FIELD

Let's piggyback on what we were just talking about, but in more detail. We live inside a torus field, on the plane of inertia in the middle. There is polarity, the positive above, the heavens, and the negative below, the underworld (or hell). Just as each of our bodies are fractally surrounded by our own individual energetic torus field, also known as our aura. The left side of our body is the negative side that takes, and the right side is the positive side that gives. That's also why we shake hands with the right hand, we are offering good energy, not trying to take it. We are told that we live on a globe, which is a half-truth, because if it were a full lie then we could see right through it, instead it is often difficult to discern something that is half true. It is a half-truth because there is a circular field that surrounds us, the torus field, although it is an energetic field. Before you call us crazy, there are just too many things that don't add up with the globe model to make sense. For instance, according to the earth curvature calculators, the earth curves 8 inches for every 1 mile. So if something is 10 miles away, the bottom 80 inches of the target should not be visible due to the curvature. Here are a few examples that you can search up for yourself that don't follow that rule: in Greece Mt. Athos from Alexandroupolis – 93 miles,

Mt. Athos from Skopelos – 77 miles, and Mt. Taygetos from Falasarna, Crete – 124 miles. I'm sure you'll argue about refraction over water, or that it disappears from view like the horizon, until of course you get a camera or telescope with powerful zoom and it reappears. The water doesn't do magical bending just so your foundation can remain true, you'll need to go watch Avatar: the Last Airbender if you want that. Water always, always, seeks level. All of these extra calculations suddenly need to be taken into account to understand why these targets can be seen over such great distances, but that doesn't follow Occam's Razor at all. Occam's Razor is a principle of logic and problem-solving that states that the simplest explanation is usually the best one. As usual, simple is better, complexity allows one to believe that there are "experts" out there that are so much smarter and have figured it out for them. That's called faith, once again, the thing science likes to make fun of religion for. Strange that. Although, if you just read the Bible it would be clear right from the beginning. This comes directly from the official Vatican Bible right on their website: Genesis 1:6-10 "Then God said, "Let there be a dome in the middle of the waters, to separate one body of water from the other." And so it happened. God made the dome, and it separated the water above the dome from the water below it. God called the dome "the sky." Evening came, and morning followed – the second day. Then God said, "Let the water under the sky be gathered into a single basin, so that the dry land may appear." And so it happened: the water under the sky was gathered into its basin, and the dry land appeared. God called the dry land "the earth," and the basin of the water he called "the seas." God saw how good it was." Genesis 1:14-18 "Then God said: "Let there be lights in the dome of the sky, to separate day from night. Let them mark the fixed times, the days, and the years, and serve as luminaries in the dome of the sky, to shed light upon the earth." And so it happened. God made the two great lights, the greater one to govern the day, and the lesser one to govern the night; and he made the stars. God set them in the dome of the sky, to shed light upon the earth, to govern the day and the night, and to separate the light from the darkness. God saw how good it was." What better way to hold a story as old as time, than in the stars, where they cannot be edited or warped by whatever empire is ruling at the time. Why is it there have always been constellations and never any more? Why is it that stars and constellations have never changed for tens of thousands of years? Sure, go ahead and argue that the distance from us to them is so vast that the difference is minute in comparison. But, we know thanks to the cave paintings found in France that the constellations have been the same for over 50,000 years. Of course, we also have to have faith and trust science that they really are so far away because we can't physically measure the distance. Why is it that every depiction of galaxies is a flat spiral? Centrifugal force is a common argument, but if that truly were the case then they would ultimately look like a ball because the stars would rotate in all different angles around their center. This of course all hinges on the theory of gravity. The same gravity that keeps the moon magically tidally locked instead of being pulled into us, but not stopping the much smaller meteors, comets, and asteroids from doing the same. There's just so many exceptions that have to be made over and over again, so many leaps of faith that must be taken to keep it status quo. It shouldn't be like that, it should be simple, uniform, and easy to understand.

The Chicxulub crater that supposedly wiped out life on the earth, where the Gulf of Mexico now is, doesn't have a huge asteroid remnant. There is just a large hole, we are supposed to believe and take it on faith that a giant asteroid caused this, and yet there is no proof of the asteroid. Where did the asteroid go? A giant rock that was allegedly 10 km. in size just disappeared? These are just some of the silly things that we're told and come to accept because no one is questioning the rationality of it. Why are there massive plateaus of mountains that look as if they've been cleanly cut? How could rocks and lava naturally cause that? That is such a leap of reality. Take Devil's Tower National Monument for example, it takes much less of a leap of reality to believe this used to be a giant tree. It looks exactly like a tree stump, just much larger, and turned to stone. (Which can happen very quickly when something is induced with a massive amount of electricity.) Our world used to be full of massive trees that we would call home. Trees form a canopy and a different biome for the things living beneath them. Look no further than a rainforest, life is extremely different below the trees than it is above. In the past when there were a lot of massive trees they would also form a canopy, this is where the idea of the "Vapor Canopy" comes from. The area underneath the trees would be subject to higher amounts of gasses, and one of those would be oxygen. More oxygen leads to bigger things, scientists have tested this with insects and the insects grow many times larger than we are used to in an environment bolstered with oxygen. So, this explains why things used to be so much larger, why we find so many skeletons of much larger animals, and humans. The largest horse skeleton was found in California, and it was 60 feet tall. (Yes, horses, lions, elephants, and many other animals all originally come from the Americas. Then we have a great deluge and they disappear and suddenly show up in Europe and Eurasia, as if they were transported by a large ship or ark, Noah's ark.) Skeletons of larger humans are found in all parts of the world. Ever wonder where the NFL teams New York Giants, or Tennessee Titans got their names from? There were so many 9 ft.+ tall skeletons found in those areas. In what was formerly called Dacia, Romania, there have been several 15 ft.+ tall human skeletons found as well. There are literally hundreds of examples, we just listed a few to get the point across, believe them or not, but you should go search for yourself and be amazed. It is important to bring up the point that everything in our timeline was much bigger and has only gotten smaller due to our environment, (which also matches our level of intellect, spirituality, and understanding of the world, very small now,) because it really wasn't all that long ago. We are talking a few thousand years to possibly even a few tens of thousands of years. Not this multiple millions of years junk that is spewed everywhere as "science." We have giant skeletons of men buried with giant animals, they were living together at the same time. Dinosaurs become a controversial subject when the timeline starts to shrink. The word dinosaur is from the Greek "deinos" (terrible) and "sauros" (lizard), so a terrible lizard. How could they know it was a terrible lizard unless they experienced it themselves? The Greek meaning of the word dinosaur sounds like it would apply a lot more to a dragon, now that would be a terrible lizard to come across. These dragons, and many other strange mythical creatures are found all over old maps dating in the 1700s and beyond. Map-makers were highly respected individuals. Kings would order maps to be made, and if something was wrong or inaccurate with the maps, that could cost the map-maker their life. So, why would they put mythical creatures in certain places of the map unless they were actually there, and instead it was a warning for whomever was going there to be aware of the dangers in that area. That time frame isn't that long ago, and it lines up pretty closely with the creation of the Smithsonian (where large skeletons were sent and never seen from again) and the big game hunting era which was also spurred on by the Smithsonian's bounties.

Now aside from Finland, America is where the real history that we are taught in our texts predominantly comes from. Aside from Finland, because of the information from the Bok Saga, and also that is where the Phoenicians originate from. The Phoenicians' history is extremely vague on purpose. If you were to compare a Phoenician ship to a Viking ship, they are almost exactly the same. The Phoenicians were the real traders from where we get the actual East India Trading company. Their trading route connections were spread the world across, and this put them in a powerful position. If you look back far enough on older maps you will find that America used to be called "India". In fact, North America was called India Superior, and South America was called India Inferior. So, when we're told that Columbus was sailing to find the East Indies, he knew exactly what he was looking for – he was searching for what we know as America. All of the conquistadors of that time were. The Conquistadors were reporting back to their kings that they were coming into contact with people that were a head or two taller than them, (so 6.5-7+ ft. tall) pale white skinned, red headed, and they spoke a language extremely similar to that of Hebrew. These were the Creek and Seminole Indians. (Seminole just means "first", and if you search up the Seminole Indian Hat you will find a square shaped hat that looks very similar to the Semitic Jew Hat.) Creek is extremely similar to the word, "Greek", now isn't it? That is no coincidence, as there are none. Ever wonder why there's so many cities in the United States that are the same as the ones in the Middle East like: Egypt – Georgia, Cairo – Georgia, Athens – Georgia, Rome – Georgia? The list goes on and on. We're told that they named these cities because of the history originating in the Middle East, but it's actually the other way around. Just like in the first chapter, everyone and everything got relocated to Europe and Asia after the Great Flood, and they named the cities in their newly settled area with the names from their original area, which was America. The largest amount of mummies found in the world come from Arizona, and after that, Colorado. All of these mummies were relocated to the Middle East by the British Empire in the late 1800s to fabricate the new historical narrative that history began in the Middle East. Because, if you're trying to look for past civilizations, and you're searching in the wrong spot, you'll never find it. It was actually an ingenious move by them. And it was the Smithsonian that tremendously helped spur this movement, because they were considered the primary institution that was contacted anytime mummies or giant human and animal skeletons were found in America. In the late 1800s, the governor of Colorado was even documented reaching out to the Federal government and begging them to intervene because the Smithsonian was taking all of their mummies, and there was no law preventing it. Cities in America are just built on top of older cities, sometimes even 3 or 4 cities built layer on top of layer. The Mississippi River was actually the real Nile River. A lot of excavating was done all up and down the Mississippi in the 1800s and they just kept finding city after city, sometimes even as far down as 100 feet below the surface were structures found. Massive underground cities were discovered in this same time period in places like Nevada, where the witnesses reported finding cities with roads in all directions that lead to even more cities. They even state they encountered 4 foot tall gnomes that were dark skinned, assumedly because they had adapted to the lack of sunlight. Even in Florida, human beings were discovered that were less than one foot tall at places like the Singing Tower at Bok Tower Gardens, which is another very interesting location to say the least. All of this may be hard to believe, but the truth is there, none of this is being made up. Don't just take our word for it, go search for yourself, but you wouldn't even begin searching until at least hearing this. Once again, fact is stranger than fiction, and stories like J.R.R. Tolkien's Lord of the Rings begins to sound a lot more real than fantasy.

So our timelines might be altered, what's the big deal? The big deal is that why would our timeline need to be altered in the first place? Ask yourself why a place like Pompeii was completely bombed for 2 straight days during WW2 because the Allies claimed that the Germans were holding ammunition there. There was, and still is, no proof that the Germans were holding ammunition there, but we'll never know. Start to look a little deeper, and you'll notice many places were bombed for no obvious war-related reasons during the World Wars quite often. And don't think it was just limited to the World Wars either. When there is a war, everything is up for grabs, and a lot of old antiquitech and history gets demolished under the guise of wars. Pompeii was also known as

Herculaneum. According to our history, we discovered Pompeii (Herculaneum) in 1763. What's strange is that there is a large stone memorial plaque on the way to Naples that lists a date of destruction for Herculaneum as 1631. How could there be a listed destruction for a town that we hadn't even discovered yet until 1763? And also according to our history, Mt. Vesuvius erupted in 79 AD and wiped out Pompeii. In fact that date is drilled into us in school, at least here in America, just like the globe. We all know that as a child we soak in the most information quickly, where our foundations start to be built, it seems fitting that we would be taught this at such a young and naive age, because otherwise it might be a much tougher pill to swallow. Additionally, have you ever found it strange how the bodies were found in Pompeii? It's like the people there didn't have more than a few seconds before the volcano eruption froze them in place. It seems hard to believe that people without our common distractions like TV, video games, phones, and even the internet couldn't realize that an eruption was about to happen, and that they needed to leave quickly. We also saw this same style of death happen much more recently, look no further than the "Maui Fires" of 2023. Strange that. (This means that the technology that did this was available as far back as the destruction of Pompeii, whenever that truly was. And there are plenty of more examples of burnt out and melted cities like: Ellora Caves – India, Ancient Caves – Granada, Longman Grottos – China, Petra, Moorish Caves – Spain, Lycean Tombs – Turkey, and the best example Uchisar Castle – Cappadocia.) Still on the topic of timeline altering, where did the steampunk era go? As an overall consciousness we all know that there was a steampunk era, and yet there isn't one in our known historical timeline. It feels like the steampunk era would slot in only a few hundred years ago, if even a little more than just 100 years ago. The steampunk era is depicted with technology that is seemingly still slightly beyond our own, but with a style of dressing that is older than our current. It's almost as if they were using technology that was on it's last legs of understanding, so to speak, while still devolving to what we are today. As if they had inherited technology that had been handed down to them, but no real idea of what made it work, just how to use it. (Seems kind of familiar to today?) That is exactly the case. That's why that era had to essentially be deleted from our history. It would bridge the gap between the last cycle, or phase of humanity, to where we are now. Instead we assume we are the smartest technologically that we've ever been. There's no way the governments and corporations would have as much control over us if we had access to the limitless free energy like they had in the steampunk era. There's no profit in that either. Think of it this way, the last and most recent time our species had access to limitless free energy was the steampunk era. If you were in control, or trying to take control, it would make all the sense in the world to wipe that from the history books to make it seem as if it didn't exist. Once a generation or 2 forgets that energy should be free, because what history can they look back on, then they begin to accept that it's not free and then you can turn them into slaves and make them work for it. This method is tried and true as old as time, countless warring countries and empires would erase or destroy the history and lineage of the conquered area. They would then replace it with their own, and after a generation or 2 their new implanted history would become the new accepted norm for that area because anyone that even knew the prior truth would have died off, or been killed, at that point anyways. Or in our most recent case, they would be put into insane asylums. Ever wonder why there used to be a ridiculous amount of insane asylums? Just giant massive buildings that were the size of universities. Almost all of them founded, in as far back as the 1700s, and yet none of them say "built". (The buildings literally say "founded" because they found it, they didn't build it. If they did, it would say "built," it's that simple. Yes we're implying these are reused and repurposed buildings that were already there.) It's as if everyone was crazy. And yet everyone complains how backwards and crazy it is today, and hardly anyone is in an insane asylum. As usual, truth is often more strange than fiction. To quote the last lines of the Chernobyl mini-series from HBO, "We are so focused on our search for truth, we fail to consider how few actually want us to find it, whether we see it or not, whether we choose to or not. The truth doesn't care about our needs or wants. It doesn't care about our governments, our ideologies, our religions. It will lie in wait for all time. And this, at last, is the gift of Chernobyl. Where I once would fear the cost of truth, now I only ask: What is the cost of lies?" This quote doesn't explicitly apply just to Chernobyl, because it is a fractal of what our governments and leaders have been doing for ages. There is a karmic debt that has to balance out, and it is finally time the truth will balance out the years of lies.

Ch. 7 SPIRITUALITY

Spirituality is a part of us as much as water is, whether we believe in religion or not. The point of life is that it has no purpose. It has to be this way because that gives us the free will to create endlessly. To give ourselves purpose. It wouldn't work any other way. Life really and truly is about the journey, not the destination. Our physical bodies die in time, but our spirit is eternal and continues on after physical death. It is our spirit that continually returns to inhabit another body cyclically, reincarnation. (There is a lot of truth to Avatar: The Last Airbender in that regard.) We plan out every life before coming down to live it out. We make contracts with our parents, our friends, our lovers and agree to teach each other in different ways. We pick all of them. In this life you may be the child, but in a past life you may have been the parent to your parent. We choose when we are going to be born, where we are going to be born. (this is why our zodiac is important because we choose to have the zodiac we have) As crazy as it may seem, some of us chose to be born into a very hard life, while others into a very easy life. Perhaps the latter had a life too easy, and wanted to see what it would be like to experience a hard life, and vice versa. We have all of time to experience everything, so it will happen eventually. The whole point of recycling is because we must learn, and it takes a long time to learn. We all come from one, from source. And as we physically die we return back to one and bring with us our memories and experiences of the past life to add to the whole, the one. From the beginning there was source, or as science calls it, a singularity. And we are full of unlimited power and potential, but like a newborn, we must learn mastery of emotions and desires. Every desire must be fulfilled otherwise you will always feel like something is missing. So, we begin from source and then fall down to experience different perspectives and desires all the while learning. Eventually, we will descend all the way to the bottom of source polarity, from completely whole and positive to completely separated and negative, to fulfill our most corrupt and wicked desires. It is from this point that we can then ascend back up all the way back to source. To end the trance, trance-end, to transcend. To ascend we have to shed our karmic debts. (The Ho'oponopono Prayer from the earlier chapter mentioned during the dry fast is a good place to start.) It makes sense that as a collective veganism and vegetarianism are on a meteoric rise. It's because there is a karmic debt incurred with eating meat, whether directly or indirectly taking life, but also the consumption of blood. Meat has always been associated with sacrifice in some form or another. Sacrifices always lead to more sacrifices, it's a vicious cycle, and our god, source, never asked for sacrifices. God is a god of giving and abundance, because that is whole, that is love. As far as we know, the first sacrifice was documented in the Bible in the story of Cain and Abel. This story is often misunderstood. It is said that Abel brought the first and best of his flock, but it never says he sacrificed any of them. In fact the word used in the Bible does not translate to sacrifice, but rather to the word "offering." Cain brought herbs, which was all there was at the time, so this was nothing new. God looked upon Abel's offering with favor because he had cultivated life that was breeding more life, creation. Our power. We all know what happened after, but it also says that when Cain slew Abel, and Abel's blood touched the ground, that God felt it and cried out. Like stated earlier, sacrifices always lead to more sacrifices. For example, if a farmer would sacrifice one lamb in hopes of a better harvest, then the next he would sacrifice two lambs in hopes of an even better harvest. More loss of life incurs, needlessly. Genesis 1:28 "God blessed them, saying "Be fertile and multiply; fill the earth and subdue it. Have dominion over the fish of the sea, the birds of the air, and all the living things that move on the earth." Like we mentioned in the previous chapters, we have dominion, but that only gives us the right to subdue, it doesn't mean that we need to kill needlessly. We simply have the right to subdue, to defend ourselves by killing a wolf, but at the same time the right to keep the chicken alive because in the long-term it provides much more food by laying eggs, than the temporary meat it serves. A wolf could never think that way about a chicken, but we can. Genesis 1:29-30 "God also said: "See, I give you every seed-bearing plant all over the earth and every tree that has seed-bearing fruit on it to be your food; and to all the animals of the land, all the birds of the air, and all the living creatures that crawl on the ground, I give all the green plants for food." And so it happened." God says explicitly here in this verse that every seed-bearing plant and seed-bearing fruit is to be our food. There could even be an argument made that perhaps the "sin" that Eve let into the world by eating the forbidden fruit in the Garden of Eden was the beginning of eating at all. While it may seem crazy to believe, there is such a thing as breatharianism, the act of not needing to eat or drink to survive. We are a long way away from that now, but that is because we have lowered our frequency so much. If we were much higher frequency as Adam and Eve were, since they were essentially 1st generation directly from source, then it could be a possibility. That would explain the beginning of the downfall to experience desire, starting with the desire to want to taste and eat food. And it was at that point we had to eat to survive from then on. But, as everything is cyclical we should return to that point in the future. To have raised our frequency to such a point that we are light and almost ethereal, more spirit than physical, we would no longer have a need for physical food or drink, and having experienced the downfall all the way to the point of rock bottom and come back up, experienced all desires and emotions and mastered them, be able to fully transcend back to oneness. This is why we must all leave meat behind and move to a more plant-based diet, and eventually to fruits. Following the order of Adam and Eve, but just in reverse: from nothing, to fruits, to all plants, to flesh (rock bottom), then back to plants, then fruit, and finally back to nothing. It sounds hard to believe, but that is what crystallization is about, 5-d (5-dimensional) Christos energy. Christos energy is the way back to crystallization, to be like Christ. We only consist of spirit, water, and salts (crystals) after all. Consider the caterpillar and butterfly. A caterpillar has the cells of the butterfly within it. But, over time the butterfly cells begin to multiply and once the threshold is crossed of more butterfly cells than caterpillar cells, a transformation occurs. There is no going back after a caterpillar has transformed into a butterfly, it is transformed forever. The same applies to us, once we transcend there is no going back, there is nothing to miss or be sad about, because to have ended the trance is to have completed the little game we are all here to play. The game called life.

Let's speak about power, because people will claim everyone seeks power, but the power they are referring to is power over others, basically the egoic desire for power. True power comes from understanding and harmonizing with the natural laws of the universe, not from dominating others. The path to true influence is through wisdom, compassion, and raising the collective consciousness. The way to bring positive change to the world is to focus on awakening others to their true nature and helping humanity evolve, which is the purpose of this book. Power over others is an illusion. True mastery comes from power over oneself and living in alignment with universal principles. Words are spells, it's literally called "spelling" for a reason, and the way things are spelled out is based on grammar, which comes from the word "grimoire" - a book of spells, magic book, or a spell book. Words have the power to influence others in positive and negative ways. It is also important to speak to yourself, and to equally be mindful of what you say about yourself because your belief creates your reality. So if you say that you are bad at cooking, then you will be bad at cooking, and vice versa. Words are so powerful, literally just saying that you are good at cooking a few times will make you better at cooking, especially if you keep at it. This applies to everything. Sometimes it's as simple as someone you respected when you were young telling you that you were good at something, and then you believed it, and then it actually became that way. So this is why affirmations are useful. We know that time is not linear, so when you say that you are thankful for something that means that you have it. Even if you don't actually have that thing yet, if you say to yourself that you are thankful that you have it you are drawing that reality closer to your reality simply because you believe it. It's that simple. It will take more or less time depending on how much is being asked for. Depending on how far away from that reality you are in relation to it is what determines how long it takes to manifest. So that's why if you say you're thankful for a mansion for just one day, it probably won't happen. Things take time to build and manifest, but as long as you keep at it you are drawing and manifesting that reality closer towards your own. It will manifest in ways that may not seem apparent, like perhaps a few months later you ended up getting a job that was triple your yearly salary, and then 5-10 years down the road you purchased what felt like a mansion to you. Because everything happens naturally, it's not an instant flash like we'd sometimes hope for it to be. But, we all know this power exists because we all know of the idea of "jinxing", which is only negative, the fear of saying something bad because it might come true. So, why not just flip that on its head and apply it positively? Whether you get the mansion the next day, or 10 years later, it still technically happened because time is only relative, not linear. But it still happened.

Lastly, let's speak about super powers, or the supernatural. We know that we used to be able to speak with animals because the Bible tells us that Adam and Eve spoke with the snake that tempted Eve. Eve wasn't like "Woah, is this snake talking to me?", she responded to the snake in the same manner she would speak with Adam, so we know that this was completely normal for them. The list of powers that we can have is only limited by our imagination. As we know, everything is cyclical, so believe it or not, at some point in the future we will actually inherit these supernatural powers again. These powers coincide with the level of frequency, and as previously discussed, we are very low frequency currently. Just compare our lives to the natural lives of Adam and Eve. The quest for enlightenment and health is the way to raise our frequency. So, it's possible to say that choosing that path could even be an incentive to get super powers sooner. We understand that might come off as a strange way to think about it, but you can't even hope to get super powers until your temple is healed and whole. Until you are in-tune with your body, mind, and spirit. And when you have become fully in-tune you will understand that anything and everything is possible because we are all source, god, with the power to create. And that belief, will leave you limitless.

Ch. 8 SUN, MOON, AND STARS

As we covered in the first chapter, the sun and the moon are both luminaries in our sky, as said so by God in the very first chapter of Genesis. The earth is not a spinning ball hurtling through an infinite vacuum, but rather a stationary plane existing within a complex toroidal energy field. The torus is a fundamental shape in the structure of the universe, representing the flow of energy in and out of a system, maintaining balance and harmony. This toroidal field is what truly governs the movements we observe in the heavens above, as well as the phenomena we experience on earth. At the center of this torus lies the earth, which acts as the grounding point for the entire system. The energy flows out from this central point, curves around in a toroidal pattern, and then flows back in. This movement creates what we perceive as day and night, the seasons, and the various celestial cycles. The primary driving force behind the movement of the celestial bodies, including the sun, moon, and stars, is the electromagnetic energy that permeates the aether. The aether is an ancient concept, often dismissed by modern science, but it is crucial in understanding the true nature of our reality. It is a subtle, all-pervading medium through which electromagnetic waves and forces travel, influencing the motion of all bodies within this plane. At the heart of this system lies the Black Sun, a powerful occult symbol (represented at the bottom of the Masonic Square and Compass symbol) representing the hidden forces or unseen energies that influence and sustain the visible world. This Black Sun is the source or engine behind the cosmic cycles, projecting the light that manifests as the Sun and Moon within the earth plane. The Sun and Moon, which are much closer and smaller than mainstream science suggests, move in circular paths above the earth (spiraling). Their paths are determined by the electromagnetic currents flowing through the aether, shaped by the toroidal field and powered by the Black Sun, causing the Sun and Moon to follow predictable patterns that have been meticulously observed by ancient civilizations for millennia. This aligns with the idea of the universe being a mental construct, where the physical manifestations we perceive are but projections from a deeper, unseen reality – one that could be understood as the Black Sun in this context. The entire structure, with its spirals and interconnected lines, could be interpreted as the flow of cosmic energy through the toroidal field that encircles and sustains all life, embodying the principles of "As above, so below" and the cyclical nature of creation and destruction. Above the earth lies the firmament, a solid and transparent dome that contains the waters above and acts as a boundary for the known world. The stars, which are not distant suns, but luminous points of light, are embedded within the firmament. Their movement is governed by the electromagnetic forces of the toroidal field. In the Northern Hemisphere, stars appear to rotate counterclockwise around Polaris, the North Star, which remains fixed at the center of the celestial dome. This movement is a result of the interaction between the toroidal field and the firmament. (The Northern Hemisphere obviously being closer to the center point, also known as Mt. Meru or Rupus Nigra, which is the gigantic magnetic lodestone, or mountain, in the very center.) However, as you move towards the Southern Hemisphere, the stars appear to rotate clockwise around a point that is not a fixed star like Polaris, but a reflection point created by the interaction between the toroidal field and the firmament. This difference in star rotation patterns is not due to the earth spinning, but rather the complex interplay of electromagnetic forces within the toroidal field that governs the movement of the stars across the firmament. The firmament itself is not static; it interacts with the electromagnetic energy, contributing to the cyclical nature of celestial events. This interaction can be observed in phenomena such as the precession of the equinoxes and the slow, gradual shift in the position of stars over time. All of this is underpinned by the principle of vibration, as stated in the Hermetic axiom, "Everything vibrates, nothing rests." The entire universe, including the earth, is in a state of constant vibration, and it is these vibrations, expressed as frequencies, that dictate the structure and movement of everything within the toroidal system. Different frequencies correspond to different energies and forces, and it is the interplay of these frequencies that creates the patterns we observe in nature. By understanding the earth as a plane within a toroidal energy field, driven by electromagnetic forces, the Black Sun, and the aether, we can again see the interconnectedness of all things, and the profound intelligence that underlies the cosmos. The Universe mirrors the life cycle of a cell, and within this cosmic cell, all creation exists within the dynamic flow of a torus. The torus represents the primal force of creation, a self-sustaining loop of energy that perpetually regenerates. Earth, as the central cymatic pattern within this torus, must align with this fundamental structure. If earth were a globe or concave, it would disrupt the balance of the torus. A spherical earth does not align with the energy flow of the torus, which requires a flat plane at its center to sustain the equilibrium of all energies that circulate. The earth realm reflects a cymatic pattern, a manifestation of sound and frequency that shapes all physical forms. These patterns naturally form on flat planes, akin to how vibrational frequencies create intricate, symmetrical patterns in sand or water. A spherical or concave shape would distort these patterns, making it impossible for them to maintain their sacred geometrical forms. "As above, so below; as within, so without." This Hermetic maxim teaches us that all planes of existence mirror each other. Just as the heavens are spread out as a vast, infinite expanse above, the earth reflects this as a flat plane below. The microcosm mirrors the macrocosm, and the celestial dome above projects onto the flat earth below, perfectly aligning with this principle. A globe model would break this symmetry, suggesting a separation between the heavens and earth rather than a unified, mirrored reality. The sacred geometrical layout of earth's design aligns with the structure of a flat plane. Ancient structures, ley lines, and energy grids all adhere to patterns that make sense only on a flat earth, directly mirroring the larger torus in which it resides. In a globe or concave model, these geometrical alignments would lose coherence, breaking the link between the physical and meta-physical aspects of our reality; therefore contradicting the esoteric truths and disrupting the divine order that sustains all existence.

The sun is a luminary of radium, while the moon is a luminary of plasma. The sun is a healing and growing energy, and it can do some miraculous things; consider Aldous Huxley who wrote in the 1940s how he had healed his eyes, while in old age, by sun-gazing with both open and closed eyes, and some eye straining. This is possible because of the radium coming from the Sun. Radium is even being used to treat certain cancers with success currently in modern medicine. It was so important that we as an overall consciousness got too scared to have any association with radium due to the "nukes" in 1945, because that really stopped us from re-understanding just how powerful it was. There are a lot of radium deposits in the United States. The state of Colorado actually has more radium than anywhere else, it's practically the radium capital of the world. And just by looking at it, it makes sense that Colorado would be filled with a healing and growing element like Radium, because it's so beautiful there. Before WW1, Germany owned all of the Radium deposits in the USA, and now you realize why the USA was incentivized to join that war against Germany. We were all taught in school that the Germans were doing experiments during both of the World Wars, but there isn't much detail on what they were experimenting with. They were obviously experimenting on many things, but one of great importance to them was their experiments with Radium. We know they were trying to make "super-soldiers", it's even depicted in our movies like: Captain America, The Avengers, and Superman. (Superman originated in 1938, which is the same time period that Captain America is depicted. Think about it, a "super" man.) Believe it or not, the Germans were going as far as to inject Radium directly into horses, which would then double in size and musculature overnight, and then taking the blood from the horses and injecting that into humans to create some version of Super Soldiers. We see this theme over and over in our movies and shows as well with the idea of a: jacked, usually green, very strong, "mutant." To name a few: Teenage Mutant Ninja Turtles (TMNT), the Hulk, and X-men. (Indirectly, as it was just all about mutants in general, but Wolverine is a perfect example aside from being green.) So, mutants are really not as much of a stretch to consider when you think about it, we've just been conditioned to believe that they're purely fantasy because of our movies and shows throughout the decades.

Now, the moon is much easier to look at, unlike the sun, and emits a ray that putrefies and decays. So if you have a wound, it's best not to show it to moonlight. Moonlight itself is actually a warm light, and can be compared with an area covered from moonlight to be a few degrees warmer. Because of the principle of "As above, so below", the moon actually reflects the plane that we live on, as you can see right on the back of this book. The same could be said for the sun, but obviously it's impossible to get a good look at it like we can with the moon. It's also too coincidental that the moon is tidally locked, while nothing else is. We're supposed to believe that the moon controls the tides, even though the moon is only out for, at most, half of the day, yet it keeps on controlling the tides even from the other side of the spinning globe. It would make more sense, on the globe, that at least the side that the moon is facing would experience tides, but nope, it somehow controls all of them. This is more jumping to belief, thus breaking Occam's Razor again. It takes much less leaps of faith to come to the conclusion that the moon doesn't actually control the tides, but rather it ebbs and flows from the ocean below to the ocean above and vice versa. We know, thanks to modern science even confirming it for us now, that there is a massive ocean underneath us bigger than all the seas above land (3x bigger actually). They claim that all of the water there is stored in some ridiculous mineral called "ringwoodite", which may as well be a magical space rock since we've never used that mineral for water before, and that it's 400 miles down. Well, we've only drilled 12 miles into the earth, how could we possibly know that it's this very specific mineral at this great depth we haven't even reached before? There are many massive whirlpools scattered all over our plane, and a few were so large that they even made it onto several old world maps. Just to name one, the Saltstaumen, off the coast of Norway, is considered the most powerful whirlpool in the known world. It is said that 110 billion gallons of water surge through the Saltstaumen every 6 hours, alternating sucking in and spouting out. (That sounds like breathing.) That's weird, it follows the exact same schedule of the tides. This is only re-confirming once again what the Bible has already told us and remains true with the "waters above, and waters below", that there was always an ocean beneath us. For example it demonstrates this quite plainly in the story of Noah and the Ark with Genesis 7:11 "In the six hundredth year of Noah's life, in the second month, on the seventeenth day of the month: it was on that day that All the fountains of the great abyss burst forth, and the floodgates of the sky were opened." The Bible confirms the ocean beneath right there, "All the fountains of the great abyss burst forth", where could the great abyss be at if it were inferred to be the opposite of the "floodgates of the sky"? Obviously from the ground, giant fountains shooting water "as above, so below". This is even depicted properly in the Noah (2014) movie with water shooting from up and out of the ground while the rain is pouring down from above simultaneously.

Our earth realm is similar to that of a Russian Doll, one enveloped by another, with all of our realm etherically contained within Mars (visually represented by the affectionately named "Great Red Spot" of Mars), and Mars is all contained within Jupiter (also represented by Jupiter's Great Red Spot), and so on; basically a cosmic egg. If we know that the earth reflected on the moon is 50,000 km in diameter, and since Mars is a magnitude larger to contain it, the size of Mars should be roughly 250,000,000 km. Don't forget these are etheric fields we're talking about, not planets, but they still have physical manifestations that are only accessible over very long cycles. Ebbing and flowing, breathing in and out as everything in the universe does; as it breathes in it constricts and we get to the smallest stage as we are experiencing now, and eventually it will breathe out and expand back up to the larger fields. "The symbolic depiction of the history of the earth in this electromagnetic universe, according to the fields that existed per period, is reflected in Greek mythology. At the beginning was "Gaia – Land" that gave birth to Uranus. Uranus – that means "the sky" was the personification of the celestial field – firmament, and ruler of the first generation on Land –

Gaia. He is one of the firstborn, the oldest of the Gods of the elements of nature and the firstborn son of Gaia – Land – Earth. Kronos – Saturn, was the leader and youngest of the first generation of titans, deities descended from Gaia and Uranus. He defeated his father, Uranus, and ruled during the mythical "golden age", until he was also defeated by his son, Zeus. Zeus – Jupiter after winning the kingship from his father Kronos according to the ancient Greek theology is the "Father of gods and humans", ruling the Gods of Olympus. Ares – Mars is the god of war and one of the Twelve Olympians, son of Hera and Zeus. Phobos and Deimos were tied to his chariot. If we decode all this then we can understand that as we go back in time, we also go a field out. Each outer field is much larger than the inner one. Now we are in the phase where a small field, the field of earth that we can see on the moon, was created within the field of Mars. That is why in mythology there was a time that the moon did not exist. That time was before the creation of our field – Earth. This does not mean that the ground – land –

Gaia did not exist. Thus, on the same ground, in a small part of a larger field a smaller one was created. Earlier the great field of Mars was created within the huge field of Jupiter, while even earlier Jupiter was created within Saturn. Even before Saturn was created and time began within the field of Uranus." (Vibes of Cosmos Book 6 – Pg 95) The stars above tell the most interesting unalterable story of all time, because where else could you put the most important story than out of reach of the empires and governments that retell history as the conquerors always do. God, source, one, knew that it had to be made just this way. Every religion stems from astrology. J.P. Morgan himself said "Millionaires don't care about astrology, billionaires do." Right now in 2024 we are experiencing a solar cycle that only happens roughly every 12,000 years, which is coincidentally the same time that mainstream science says that we pass through the "photon belt." Photons are light, light in its highest frequency is love. That is a symbol of transformation for not just us, but for our entire realm. If that isn't enough, Sedna the dwarf planet, which gets its name from the myth symbolizing transformation, is also making its orbit right now; and it's on an 11,400 year cycle. What are the odds that both of those are happening right now? There are no coincidences. That is why all of the "doomer" apocalyptic talk is folly, because it's based upon apocalypses that were recorded in the past. The point of an apocalypse is misunderstood, it's a cyclical event that must occur to clear out the lower frequency to make room for the new higher frequency coming in. Each apocalypse building upon another to continually and exponentially raise the frequency. Resulting in a threshold eventually being reached that we are coming to right now. A threshold where everything is transforming into a higher frequency and transcending. So, this evolution cannot be entirely based on the past, because it is not like the past apocalypses. For those hoping for a miraculous rapture or something along those lines, that is not exactly how this works. We can look directly from the mouth of Jesus for our answer on this via the

Gospel of Thomas (which is just a collection of all the words Jesus said in the Bible), Gospel of Thomas 113: "His disciples said to Him, "When will the Kingdom come?" < Jesus said,> "It will not come by waiting for it. It will not be a matter of saying 'Here it is' or 'There it is.' Rather, the Kingdom of the Father is spread out upon the earth, and men do not see it." An apocalypse is the end of an era. An era lasts anywhere from 1,000 to 2,100 years (the same time as a zodiacal age). Which is likely why we are experiencing one now as we leave the Age of Pieces and enter the Age of Aquarius. There is also something to be said about the ending of the Age of Pieces, (or Kali Yuga – in Hinduism the Kali Yuga is considered to be the worst, shortest, and fourth yuga in the Yuga cycle. It is an age of conflict, and sin, and is believed to be characterized by a decline in the physical and moral state of humanity which is characterized as: an age of darkness, a loss of spiritual abilities – mental clarity and understanding, a belief in fixed matter – matter is fixed and absolute and religious truths were absolute definitions, physical labor – activity was directed towards physical ends, rituals – religious activity took the form of rituals, sacrifices, and prayers, and lastly ignorance – people were ignorant of their ability to change, and there were widespread attempts to destroy knowledge.) because although the exact amount of years is arbitrary, Pieces is a "mutable" zodiac sign. During mutable and cardinal zodiacal signs there is too much change occurring, which is part of the natural process of life. But, once a fixed zodiacal sign is reached, like Aquarius, a "golden age" can occur because there is no more changing and molding. And we can see this depicted evidently by Pieces being a sign that is about top-down power and withholding knowledge and information, while Aquarius is about grass-roots power from the bottom-up and all knowledge and secrets coming to the surface; truth in all facets revealed. When it says in the Bible, or even just old ancient texts, that certain things will last "forever", we have misunderstood what the original word "forever" means. Etymology is very important, and when further examining the root of the word "ever" you will find that "ever" actually just means the length of an age, or era. So when these ancient texts say "forever," it literally means for an entire age, or era, not eternally like we've confused it with. So we have ended our current "ever", or era, and have all of this astrology lining up perfectly to reflect a great transformation, only further proving that it is the most exciting time to be alive here and now. Whether you believe it or not, everyone that is here right now chose this time to be alive to experience this. They either knew consciously or subconsciously before reincarnating that this was an event that they didn't want to miss. Why do you think our population is the biggest it's ever been? Everyone wants to see what is going to happen during this transformation event and experience it in some way for their journey. It may seem like the end for some, and a beginning for others as we are all on our own separate journeys and experiencing time in our own relative ways. For those ending their trance it may feel like this is an end that they are experiencing, but to others that are less along in their journey, they may have many more lifetimes to continue learning. But, because time is relative, when they also come to that point, this point for some of us, it will feel like we all experience it at the same time. It may be difficult to wrap your mind around that, but it's because it's so difficult to not think of time linearly.

We already know that everything is connected, and the principle "As above, so below" fractally permeates everywhere as well, so we find there are metals that represent our luminaries like gold representing the sun, and silver representing the moon. Gold is a solar metal, and silver is a moon metal. These are very conductive metals, and we are electrical beings. Once again, this is why royalty would not only wear, but use gold and silver to eat and drink with. Not only would it clean the food and drink, but it would electrify it and that would restructure it with higher frequencies. Copper is another metal which does this well, and it's also well-known for its anti-inflammatory benefits. It is a lot more affordable, and is also commonly worn for these reasons. Currently in India, the people there have no choice but to drink from the highly polluted Ganges River. They draw water from the Ganges River with copper vessels and let it sit for at least 24 hours which helps to clean the water. Obviously, it's not ideal, but they're making the best of what they have, and they're still alive. Even tin can be used to clean and restructure water to a degree, and that's why soldiers were given tin cans during the World Wars, and other wars, to drink out of. Unfortunately, that consideration has been left behind, and the new standard has become plastic. Once again, we are demonstrating the attack on our bodies from every angle, and the lack of knowledge and care of overall health. But, we are the smartest our species has ever been, right?

Lastly, it is said that Antarctica is a continent, but in reality it is a large ice wall that is sheltering us from the further surrounding continents and islands that are clearly displayed via the reflection of our plane by the moon. You can think of it as a sort of frequency barrier that encloses our area to allow it to be the smallest it could possibly be, so that we could get down to the lowest frequency we've ever known. But, this is just the way things have to be to match our low frequency and consciousness, and eventually they will melt and allow us the freedom, if we so choose, to re-discover the surrounding lands as our consciousness simultaneously rises back up as well. Not only will Antarctica open, but the North Pole, the center, Rupes Nigra, which has also been energetically barred to us for a time, will re-open to us and others may prefer to move inward towards it instead, as it will be, and always has been, emanating the highest frequency outwards like a drop of water causing ripples. (This is why all the "elites" are so insistent about moving to "Mars." They need to escape the higher frequencies emanating from the center point, or risk death due to their current extremely low frequency life cycle. Which, to be fair, is just a natural stage of their journey at this current time, as we all also experienced our own similar stage at some point because of our each individual journeys that consist of reincarnating and experiencing life and desires in every different way to eventually learn everything we needed to and master our desires and emotions in this long game called life, and transcend.) One last thing, the perpetual sunlight observed in Antarctica is often considered a way to prove that the earth is a globe, but that is not the real reason there is perpetual sunlight there. The reason for perpetual sunlight can most easily be explained by using the caustic coffee cup example. In optics, a caustic is a curve of concentrated light, defined as the envelope of light rays reflected by a curved surface – the firmament, or dome, above. Another example of the caustic coffee cup would be a rainbow. So, the Sun luminary focal point is reflecting off the firmament and therefore causing perpetual sunlight in this location, this further solidifies that we live under a firmament, just like God told us in the very first book of the Bible.

Ch. 9 GROUNDING

Grounding really is so simple, and yet it's so underused. We are electrical beings that build up charge, and grounding releases that charge. Grounding also increases blood flow throughout the body in as little as a few minutes. Now, barefoot grounding not only increases blood flow, but it also strengthens the feet. Feet are your foundation, they're what your whole body sits upon, and unfortunately they have become extremely overlooked. How can one expect to have a strong body or mind when their foundation is poor? When it comes to feet, our society has become reliant upon shoes. Sure, shoes have a purpose, and that's where having a wooden staff can be a substitute for not having bare feet on the ground. Why else do you think every druid or wizard is depicted with a wooden staff? So they remained grounded even while wearing sandals, or shoes. The sandals in the past were at least stiff and strong, so the user still needed to have a strong foot sole. (Just think about the word "sole", it sounds just like the word "soul", and that is no coincidence – our sole needs to have a good foundation just as our soul does.) But, in our modern age there is so much cushion between our sole and the ground. We can thank Nike for starting that, and the cushioning has just gotten bigger and bigger since then. Not only that, but the material used on the bottom of the shoe is usually a good electrical insulator, so there's no chance of any grounding happening regardless. But, these overly-cushioned shoes have created an even larger problem – people don't have proper running gaits anymore. When there's so much cushion, and that's the only way you've ever known, the average person tends to run on their heels; heel-striking the ground. They don't know any better because the cushion is making them think it's not that bad, but the damage is actually immense. Of course, this problem would never have even occurred if they had ever tried running barefoot, because good luck running with your heel striking the ground first while barefoot, it's quite painful and not to mention extremely unnatural. If you let a young child run barefoot they would run the proper way immediately, because it's a completely natural thing. It's a shame that people are so sedentary and lazy now that they've been conditioned and learned the wrong way to run. Listen how simple that is, they literally do not know how to run. We have a beautifully designed body, and the foot and ankle work together to create a natural cushion, like a rubber-band, for the body while running. If you run instead by heel-striking, even while wearing these largely cushioned shoes, there is no rubber-band effect happening and so your knees and spine are compressing every single time your foot is hitting the ground. Every single strike is doing a little bit of damage, which compounds over years. So as you get older, you not only have weak feet, but an improper gait that has been slowly destroying your spine and knees. An absolute recipe for failure. And, all of this could have been avoided by simply going outside barefoot every once and awhile (the more the better obviously), and occasionally even jogging or running around in the grass or dirt. This would have bolstered your foundation, given you a healthy and proper gait, and increased the blood flow all throughout your body so you heal and repair even faster. It is absolutely so ridiculously simple, and yet here we are having to speak about it – a classic example of common sense not being common. Now just imagine being grounded at all times. Not long ago most of the homes people lived in had wooden or cement floors, both of which are conductive, so even while sleeping they were grounding. Compare that to today, where you might be lucky enough to have a grounding sheet to remain grounding while asleep, but otherwise even if you are actively grounding outside it's only for a brief period relative to the 24 hours in the day. It kind of makes you wonder why we've phased out wooden homes, which everyone knows last a lot longer, with these more cheaply made ones that don't even last as long. Additionally, we have the removal of lead paint. The narrative for the removal of lead paint in our homes is due to the worry of infants consuming the lead-based paint chips. Do you really believe that they rid our world of lead-based paint just because they were worried about infants eating paint chips? Lead-based paint blocks Electromagnetic frequencies. A perfect example of well-known harmful electromagnetic frequencies are x-rays, cell phones, and the 5G towers. With the removal of lead-based paint we have further prevented protection of constant electromagnetic frequencies from bombarding our bodies and minds even in our homes. (A quick aside on the cell phones, they emit so many harmful electromagnetic frequencies constantly – we see alarming rates of cancer occurring in the younger generation around the waist area, where they keep their phones. Never sleep next to your phone at night, and it is ideal to put your phone into airplane mode while sleeping.) And sure, it would make it difficult to have WiFi in a lead-based paint home, but then again we live in a very unnatural age.

Another simple issue of health that needs to be addressed is in our commonly used toothpaste. The toothpaste that almost everyone uses contains fluoride. A simple search on fluoride will have you believe it's harmless because it's in our water reservoirs, but actually we only began putting fluoride into our water reservoirs less than 100 years ago in 1939 thanks to a scientist that was not a doctor, nor a dentist, named Gerald J. Cox. Cox was appointed to his position by a man named Andrew Mellon who was a businessman and banker who was also the Secretary of the Treasury, and as Secretary of the Treasury he was also in charge of the U.S. Public Health Services at that time. Andrew Mellon also led the company ALCOA, which had found a way to cut costs on disposing of fluoride by essentially depositing it into our water supply. This is where Mellon needs to find some excuse to make it reasonable to do. That's when Mellon appointed the scientist Gerald J. Cox to change the image of fluoride with his claim that it is "good for our teeth." The following year, the military backed Mellon's company,

ALCOA, because they also wanted to profit from this toxic substance, and the rest is history. Fluoride is more toxic than lead, but slightly less toxic than arsenic. Fluoride is also the same chemical used to enrich uranium for nuclear weapons and prepare Sarin nerve gas, so now you see why the military had an incentive to join the fluoride disposal business, and disgustingly even turn a profit on it. Fluoride does not improve your teeth and actually can degrade them even more, so you also see here why the dentist is incentivized to push this narrative because that means more repeat customers. Fluoride in the drinking water causes a condition called dental fluorosis, which is a discoloration of the tooth enamel that leads to white patches becoming discolored and going from yellow, to orange, and then brown. Scientific studies show that fluoride is neurotoxic and causes birth defects and osteoporosis. Not only that, but fluoride can also include damage to the immune, digestive, and respiratory systems. Fluoride also affects the kidneys, liver, brain, and the thyroid. Fluoride can also increase the risk of hip fractures in the elderly, and the risk of osteosarcoma. And most importantly, fluoride calcifies the pineal gland, which is an endocrine gland that sits between the two hemispheres of the brain and handles the synthesis and secretion of melatonin. So, this chemical is in both our drinking water, and toothpaste, and since our government genuinely doesn't care about our health it's our job to take preventative actions. Your water must be filtered from fluoride, whether you decide to use a natural spring, or purchase a water filter that specifically says it also filters fluoride. And you must no longer use toothpaste that contains fluoride. Every time you brush your teeth you swallow roughly 5% of the toothpaste. Now multiply that for every day, or possibly even twice a day, by 365 for every day of the year, and then multiply that for the years you've been alive. That's an unsettling amount of fluoride just from the toothpaste alone, before even considering the water. Despite what you may think, it's actually very easy to make toothpaste, and very affordable. There are many different ways to make it and it's very easy to search up, but here is one that we use ourselves that makes a very large amount, and the amounts can easily be doubled or tripled, etc.

How to make your own natural toothpaste:

    1 - 6 tablespoons Xlear: Xylo-Sweetner (this is just xylitol, any brand will do)
    2 - 2 teaspoons of Peppermint Extract
    3 - ½ cup of Baking Soda
    4 - ¼ cup of Coconut Oil. Simply mix and stir until it turns into a slimy sludge
    5 - store inside anything. (we recommend mason jars)

It will not come as a surprise, but fluoride is not the only thing that harms our teeth, nor is it even the worst offender. The worst offender would be the average diet. But, believe it or not, fruits do not cause any harm to your teeth. A diet of only fruits, fruitarian, would technically mean that you'd never even have to brush your teeth. This makes even more sense in relation to our historical timeline, how brushing has become such an accepted way of life because of our poor diets, and that it didn't used to be this way. Adam and Eve certainly weren't brushing their teeth in the garden, because there was no need.

Now another health fallacy needs to be addressed and that is the one about germs and viruses. The mainstream belief in viruses and germ theory suggests that tiny particles – viruses and bacteria – are the primary causes of disease. This notion is deeply embedded in the fabric of modern medicine. Viruses, as they are commonly understood, are not autonomous entities that invade and destroy the body. Rather, what are called "viruses" are misunderstood processes of the body itself – detoxification efforts on a cellular level. When the body undergoes stress or encounters toxic environments, it initiates a process of cleansing. What is observed under a microscope as a "virus" is often just cellular debris, the remnants of the body's natural attempt to heal and restore balance. Germ Theory, popularized by figures like Louis Pasteur, assumes that microorganisms are the root cause of disease. However, Pasteur's contemporary, Antoine Bechamp, proposed an alternative view known as terrain theory. According to the theory, the health of the body's internal environment, or "terrain," determines whether disease manifests. Germs do not cause disease; instead, they thrive in an already diseased environment. Pasteur himself is said to have acknowledged on his deathbed that "the microbe is nothing, the terrain is everything." Sickness and disease are not external forces attacking the body, but are reflections of internal imbalances – physical, emotional, mental, and spiritual. The human body is a manifestation of the soul's energy field. When this energy field is disturbed by stress, negative emotions, or toxic environments, the physical body responds with what we perceive as illness. This response is not an attack, but a message, a signal that there is a need for realignment with the natural flow of universal energy. When the body is overloaded with toxins – whether from food, water, air, or even thoughts – it initiates a detoxification process. This process can manifest as symptoms of disease, but these are not signs of a malfunction. Rather, they are evidence that the body is attempting to cleanse and heal itself. The mind and body are deeply interconnected. What you believe, think, and feel can manifest physically. Illness can be seen as a projection of unresolved conflicts, fears, or trauma within the psyche. Healing, therefore, must occur on all levels – body, mind, and spirit. Fear is a powerful force that can lower your vibration, making the body more susceptible to imbalance and dis-ease. The fear of germs and disease perpetuated by society only serves to reinforce a cycle of sickness. By shifting your perception away from fear and towards understanding and love, you raise your vibration and align yourself with the natural harmony of the universe. True health is not found in battling imaginary external threats, but in cultivating internal balance and harmony. To achieve this one must nurture the body by consuming pure, natural foods, breathe clean air, drink pure water, and avoid toxins in all forms – especially alcohol. Heal the mind by releasing fear, stress, and negative emotions; instead embrace positive thoughts and cultivate a mindset of peace and love. And finally, align with spirit by engaging in practices that connect you with the One Mind, Source, like mediation, prayer, and communion with nature. Listen to the inner voice of the soul, for it knows the path to wholeness. By understanding sickness and disease as signals from the body's inner intelligence, you can begin to view them not as enemies, but as allies guiding you back to your true, balanced state of being. This is the path of enlightenment, the way to true health, and the realization that you are the creator of your reality. Thus, the power lies within you – it always has, and always will.

Now let's talk about another overlooked health issue, body odor. Today, we just lather on deodorant and shower very frequently because the average person smells badly. We smell so badly because of our diets, especially meat. Our armpits are another area that expels toxins, and when we use deodorant to suppress this the toxin has no choice but to go inward, towards the breasts and lymph nodes. The lymph nodes in the armpit are called the axillary lymph nodes. They are part of the lymphatic system, which helps the body fight infections. So we are sending toxins back into an area whose job it is to help fight infections, therefore lowering the body's ability to fight infections. Not only that, but most deodorants are filled with heavy metals that are also going to be absorbed into the body in a very susceptible location, right on the lymph nodes. Of course, you can find healthier and cleaner deodorants free of heavy metals, but that is still just band-aiding the foundational problem – the diet. The body is literally signaling you to let you know there is a problem going on via the bad smelling body odor. It shouldn't be this way. We are not saying to not shower, nor use deodorant. But, by cleaning up your diet you will no longer produce a bad smelling body odor, so there is nothing to suppress. Transitioning to a diet of vegetables and fruits, or even just fruits, would mean no more need for deodorant. Showering would just entail taking a dip into the ocean, river, or lake – as they did not so long ago in our past. On the topic of fruits, some of the healthiest and best fruits are those with a rind, especially oranges. The rind of the fruit naturally protects it from pesticides and other sprays, it's almost as if God knew. Oranges are the literal solar representation. The depictions of the Garden of Eden have them pulling an apple to eat from the Tree, but that was actually changed and warped by the Vatican. Believe it or not, the original fruit that was taken from the Tree in the Garden of Eden was the orange, not the apple. Hilton Hotema was a writer from the late 1800s who wrote about consciousness and health and he actually ended the last few decades of his life consuming exclusively oranges. Now, we're not saying you have to be that extreme, but it's meant to invoke the power of the orange. It's that delicious and healthy that it can be exclusively consumed, and it's that succulent that it began the initial temptation and desire for Eve to consume it.

Ch. 10 THE KEYS TO A GOOD LIFE

Yeah, we know, so many people claim to have the answer or keys to life. And honestly it's not that complex, our society loves to over complexify everything and complexity tends to lead to stress. With that logic, it makes more sense that life is actually quite simple, and beautiful in it's simplicity. While we're not going to claim we have all the answers, as everyone is on their own journey, there are a few key principles, that if applied to your life, will steer you in the right direction. Obviously this book is about health and maintaining a healthy temple both physically and mentally, but you must also do something with that health. You must be active. You must exercise your body at least a few times every single week. What type of exercise is completely up to you, but with a healthy body the options are limitless. Sedentary life is unnatural and creates a vicious loop. Swim, run, weight train, find a sport or martial art. These are just a few things, but it definitely helps to do something that has progression so that the results can keep you motivated over the long-term. Because life is a marathon, not a sprint. There should be no reason that you cannot continue your preferred form of exercise for decades, assuming you take a practical approach. To maintain a healthy body physically also translates to maintaining a healthy mental, or mind. They are pretty synonymous, not 100%, but to remain active often takes discipline, and discipline helps all facets of your life. Not to mention the body wants to be active, there's a reason the body releases hormones after you exercise that make you feel good as it's also trying to foster a healthy cycle by giving us a reward, or incentive. The physical strain that exercise puts on the body also forces the body to heal faster. And that proves yet again how amazing our bodies really are. For example, let's say a machine is built to do work for 3 days a week, and if the machine is forced to work 5 days a week instead it will be more likely to fail, and the lifespan of the parts will dramatically decrease. Whereas if humans exercise 3 days a week, and then decide to shift to 4 or 5 days of exercise a week, the body adapts to the higher workload. Sure you might be a little more tired from doing more days of exercise, but there is a lot more volume being added, and yet the body amazingly responds by just adapting and handling the new amount of workload. 5 days of exercise may have been difficult the first week, but by the 3rd or 4th week it has normalized. In another example with martial arts – training jiu jitsu 1 day a week may be exhausting at first, but then you decide to move to 2 days a week and it feels just as exhausting as 1 day a week. But you've doubled your volume? Now move that to 3 days a week. Initially it's still exhausting as the body is starting to adapt, but after a few weeks of the consistent 3 days of training, the 3 days of jiu jitsu are the same level of exhausting as the original 1 day a week of training. How can that be possible? We've tripled our workload and feel the same level of exhaustion that we felt initially with only 1 day a week. We're demanding more from our bodies and it seems to just keep coming. And soon 3 days of jiu jitsu feels quite easy on the body. By expending more effort, as humans, we can almost magically get a better result, and instead the machines cannot adapt and will just reach failure sooner. That's simply incredible. We do not give ourselves credit that we're so much better than machines. We are made in God's image, the machines aren't. Additionally, something that is not to be overlooked is stretching. As we exercise we are usually contracting which leads to tightness, and then pain, and sometimes even failure due to compromise. We have to maintain a balance to counter the contractions, and this is where we find the opposite end of the spectrum, stretching. Chiropractors and massages are a huge industry for a reason, because we do not do enough stretching ourselves. We are then relying on an outside source to heal our bodies, when we always have everything we need inside. Stretching would be the opposite of contracting, and in our society we are often very contracted due to high levels of sedentariness. The word sedentary comes from the Latin word "sedere", which means "to sit." Sitting for long periods leads to contraction, or tightness, all over the body. We already need to stretch just to counterbalance the amount of sitting we do, and then if you exercise, like you should be, that adds another layer of stretching that needs to be done. This is why we see large bodybuilders that can barely move, and yet they spend a lot of money going to chiropractors and getting massages. You cannot expect to fully appreciate life if you're not flexible. So, stretching should be done weekly as well. If you do not know what to stretch or where to begin, there are so many videos out there. But, as to where to begin, the easiest place to begin is by stretching the hamstrings. The hamstrings link everything together like a chain, and they take the most strain from a sedentary lifestyle of sitting. If your calves are tight, it's likely related to your tight hamstrings. If your lower back is tight, it's probably related to your tight hamstrings. So just search for hamstring stretches and start there. Stretching the hamstrings will naturally release the hips as well, and allow you to perform a squat where your heels are on the ground, which was the natural way of pooping in the past, and still is in some countries around the world. Believe it or not, even the male body should be able to perform a split. That level of flexibility should be natural to everyone, and yet the average person is so incredibly far from being able to do that, let alone even able to perform a natural deep squat. We have also learned that there is a threshold of time that a stretch needs to be held, statically, to be considered effective and that will also lead to progressive results. That threshold is 2 minutes. 2 minutes is the minimum time a static stretch needs to be held to get the muscle to relax and start building more and more flexibility. Of course feel free to go past that, but at least reach the minimum time. Flexibility not only does the obvious of making you more flexible, but it's a form of exercise and strain on the muscle that cannot be done any other way, and therefore helps strengthen your overall foundation.

Let's address alcohol and start with what Jesus himself said about it - Gospel of Thomas 28: Jesus said, "I took my place in the midst of the world, and I appeared to them in the flesh. I found all of them intoxicated; I found none of them thirsty. And my soul became afflicted for the sons of men, because they are blind in their hearts and do not have sight; for empty they came into the world, and empty too they seek to leave the world. But for the moment they are intoxicated. When they shake off their wine, then they will repent." This is pretty straightforwardly saying that with alcohol you cannot be enlightened. Alcohol is a poison, why would you ever want to put poison into your temple on purpose? Your body must stop doing all of its natural processes and immediately address the poison that you consciously chose to put into your system, as if it didn't have enough toxin build-up from our diets that it's already trying to address any time it gets a chance. Strange that our society is so infatuated with alcohol. We've been conditioned to believe that something cannot even be celebrated without the inclusion of alcohol. Now that's some real propaganda. Why the constant need to escape this reality? Especially relative to a celebration, maybe you just won something, and that was in this reality, and now to celebrate this victory in this reality you consume alcohol to escape it? Where does that make any sense at all? To those who say they "enjoy" alcohol, you are not addressing the real reason why you enjoy it, especially if you say that you actually enjoy the taste. No, you have learned to "enjoy" the taste because you have associated it with the reality escapism that comes along with it. An argument that people make for some usefulness of alcohol is that they begin to open up, and you can see the "real" them. We counter that by arguing why are people so often hiding the real them? Why not be the authentic real "you" at all times? People don't like to hear the truth often because it hurts. But, that is for them to deal with, for "the truth will set you free." An argument can even be made for bullying to an extent. Obviously it can get out of hand, but a lot of times it can be a form of constructive criticism. Take for instance when someone calls someone else "fat", that would be classified as a form of bullying. But, it's up to the person on the receiving end to do something about it. Will they play the victim, or will they make a change? Clearly that person was called fat because they weren't skinny, so perhaps that could be the opportunity to work on no longer being fat instead of worrying that someone called you fat and doing nothing about it. Because if you actually weren't fat, and someone called you fat, it would not affect you. In our current society we are so worried about being judgment free and not offending others. Look at where that's gotten us, we are the unhealthiest we've ever been. We have the proof right in front of our eyes to see where judgment-free takes us, and it's not good. People love to bring Jesus into the equation when this topic is brought up because of him saying essentially that only he (Jesus) can judge, because he's "perfect."

Well, like we mentioned earlier in the book, the point of Jesus was to create leaders that are Christ-like. So, to be Christ-like is to judge. Judgments need to be made. This whole "only God can judge me" is just a cop out. We all need to hold each other accountable, to a high standard. Obviously to judge you must also hold yourself to a high standard, but that is the point of enlightenment. We all rise together. Jesus was accredited for doing miracles, but that was because people believed he was capable of doing miracles. Our belief creates our reality. When Jesus went back to his hometown and they only knew him as a carpenter, he could no longer do those miraculous things because they believed he was just a regular man – and their belief created that reality. Book of Thomas 31: Jesus said, "No prophet is accepted in his own village; no physician heals those who know him." Jesus has become this larger than life anthropomorphic being because people believed that he was. But, we all have that same ability, because we are all man just like him.

Laughter is something of a high frequency. Typically when you're laughing you are enjoying yourself or having a good time. Interesting that comedians have become less and less able to joke about certain topics. Comedy is not supposed to be taken seriously, and yet the comedians are sometimes harshly judged for a joke in our current modern society. This is another symptom of our judgment-free mentality that we've tried to instill. And if a joke really affects you that much, that really says a lot about your inner-self, and that needs to be addressed and worked on. Anyways, it is commonly said amongst those who are close to death that they wished they had laughed more. It has even been proven that laughter can heal illnesses, because it all starts inside, and therefore raising the frequency breaks that vicious low frequency cycle that feeds itself . So, we need to laugh more. Everyone associates and assumes the wisest of monks are very stern and serious. It's actually quite the opposite, they tend to be the funniest of beings. High levels of wisdom lead to not taking yourself so seriously. Believe it or not, when channeled beings that claim to be from the 6th and 7th dimensions talk about what life is like for them, they say it is extremely funny and full of laughter. That is because to reach those higher dimensions means you are of a very high frequency, and genuine laughter is a very high frequency. In order of lowest frequency to highest:

- nothingness – the lack of caring at all
- lust
- pain
- victimization
- suffering
- shame
- guilt
- fear
- anger
- control
- power
- will - the threshold crosses here from low to high frequency

- gratitude
- appreciation
- joy
- love
- freedom
- bliss
- wholeness

Notice how low in frequency victimization is, even below suffering. We can always choose to cultivate our own frequency because it all starts from within, "As within, so without, as above, so below." Your frequency radiates out, so if you are angry, others will pick up on that vibration; just as they will if you are happy. Do not think it just stops at people, it radiates to everything around you. People are primarily water. So, the drink you drink will be affected, the food you eat will be affected, whatever you consume will be affected. Be mindful of your mood, vibration, frequency, when you are consuming because as we've said plenty of times now, you are what you eat – and if you are consuming something that is low frequency then it will just lower your frequency even more. If there is a fight going on at the dinner table, believe it or not, that will affect everyone's food and drink. It's best to either resolve the situation and bring back up the frequency, vibration, or just for-go consuming. Generally, it's better to go without consuming anyways as fasting has been proven to extend our lifespans and health markers. So, you'll be fine without your one meal. And less meals will give you a better appreciation for what you consume, because it should never be a chore. Obviously never live to eat, but you should always enjoy what you eat. There's a reason people like to get together to eat – assuming you enjoy the company you are with, the good times of laughing and joking together at the table are a high frequency vibration that is imparted to the food and drink and make the overall experience even more enjoyable. That's how it's always meant to be. You should always be enjoying your life, we are living in heaven right now, it's just all your perspective – it's a journey, not a sprint, and it's all about the journey. Alan W. Watts said it best: "Let's suppose that you were able every night to dream any dream that you wanted to dream. And that you could, for example, have the power within one night to dream 75 years of time. Or any length of time you wanted to have. And you would, naturally as you began on this adventure of dreams, you would fulfill all your wishes. You would have every kind of pleasure you could conceive. And after several nights of 75 years of total pleasure each, you would say "Well, that was pretty great." But now let's have a surprise. Let's have a dream which isn't under control. Where something is gonna happen to me that I don't know what it's going to be. And you would dig that and come out of that and say "Wow, that was a close shave, wasn't it?" And then you would get more and more adventurous, and you would make further and further out gambles as to what you would dream. And finally, you would dream... where you are now. You would dream the dream of living the life that you are actually living today."

Ch. 11 ITS NOT DOOMSDAY

Despite everything that's being pushed in the news, it is not doomsday. To think that we're so special that only our generation would experience the "end of times" is a bit narcissistic. Once again, the news is just n.e.w.s – nothing even worth saying. It is wise to realize the age shift that is upon us though. There are omens everywhere. But, everything is actually going according to plan, God's plan, our plan, they're one in the same because we are source, we are all God. Being aware of the times is important because nothing should throw you out of balance. People will argue "How does knowing this or that impact my life?" It will impact your life for two reasons: to realize all the lies we have been told on every level, and to not be shocked by seemingly "crazy" events. So you will not be worried about an alleged war outbreak, a virus outbreak, or a child trafficking ring. You may observe them, but don't let them affect you. We are always being tempted and tested in various ways, and they are merely tests to see if we will fall victim to our emotions and get worried. This is the best time to be alive for several generations, if not hundreds. We all reincarnated at this time to experience this. You can almost never tell in the moment, but instead by looking back on it, and it would seem that 2020 was our lowest low. We had to hit our lowest low so that now we can go to our highest high. This theme has been repeatedly brought up in the book because we really want to instill that everything is ok, it's actually better than that, everything is awesome. We are experiencing truth re-surfacing in every facet and it simply couldn't be more exciting. That's why there's so many people alive today. There's no fear of global warming, just as there wasn't any fear of global freezing a few decades ago. The global warming narrative is a part of the eugenics plan. And yes, that is a very real plan. These elites think they can fool us into believing that it's getting too hot because there's too many people on this plane. First off, no matter the awful damage that we do to our home, earth, it always heals. That is not an excuse to continue doing it, but the earth is much more resilient than we give it credit for. Look no further than the giant garbage patch that is floating in the Pacific Ocean. Now there are bacteria that are feeding off the plastic in this giant garbage patch because we as a species couldn't figure out how to fix the problem ourselves. And secondly, we have more than enough land to grow food for the population that we have. Believe it or not, our food economy is completely controlled. The small country of the Netherlands is the second largest exporter of agricultural products in the world. That should be enough proof of how much food can be provided on such a small area of land. So, it's no surprise that we've treated our home badly for the past several hundred years, but that was just part of our learning cycle. The earth doesn't hold it against us, just as you wouldn't hold something against a 1 year old infant, they, we, didn't know any better. Now we do. There's a reason that growing within our social consciousness is a movement to take better care of our earth. We're finally moving past that immature and childish stage and progressing back onto track towards reconnecting with source. There's a reason small grass-roots groups are springing up across the world to reclaim and protect the ley lines that make up the spiritual grid all over our plane. We are moving towards not just any healing, but a wholesome holistic unified healing of everything at the same time, and that is the reason for this book. People are ready to heal, ready to learn the truth, they just need to be guided. And if we weren't here to guide, then we would be looking for someone to guide us. It's just the natural thing to do. We are just bringing the old wisdom back full circle because it has been hidden and warped for so long, and that finally ends now. This is for posterity. We all rise together.

Ch. 12 (1MAD) Lifestyle and the EZ-28 Challenge

Now in this book we've brought up fasting a lot, because this is everyone's ticket to self-healing everything. Full regeneration coming from the inside. It is important to incorporate fasting into your lifestyle; it shouldn't be a chore, but as necessary as getting exercise. If you fasted even 1 day every week for the entire year, that's 52 days of fasting. 52 days of healing, and not to mention 52 days that you didn't have to spend money on food. Choose a day that works best for your schedule, perhaps a day that you are quite busy to distract yourself from the pattern of eating you've created for yourself since birth. There is no question it will not be easy at first, but what is ever worth doing if it is easy? Get rid of those belief systems that if you don't eat you will be low on energy, that you can't exercise or do work while fasted. It may seem like that at first, because we've been wrongfully taught that we need food for energy, and therefore you believe that, and your belief creates your reality. But, that is a belief that is as malleable as the wind, understand and believe now that you do not need to eat to have energy. You do not need to eat to exercise or exert energy. Do not believe that you need a ridiculous amount of grams of protein to put on muscle. Look at gorillas, they only eat vegetables and they are way more muscular than we are. Yes we are not gorillas, but muscle is muscle. And especially get rid of this notion that you need to eat many meals a day. You should only eat 1 meal a day (1-M.A.D.), or at most 2. Just eating one meal a day will really build your appreciation for food because you will definitely be sure that you like what you're going to eat because that's your one meal for the day. It also allows you to take more care into what you are going to eat. It's a lot easier to spend time preparing your meal if it's going to be your only meal for the day. Often we get lazy when preparing meals because in the back of our mind we know that we're going to eat more meals throughout the day. We will still have the same muscle mass after swapping to eating one meal a day and not worrying about protein; and especially without eating any meat at all. These were all belief systems that our society taught us to think were the only ways to build muscle, and maintain it. It turns out, that's not true. Once you realize that, and you change your belief system, you will realize you can still workout and exercise and look "healthy" or even "muscular" while only eating fruits and vegetables and only one meal a day. It's your one meal of the day, so make it a great meal and enjoy until you're full. Even enjoy a dessert if you wish. Because if you make eating too strict you will end up rebounding and resenting it. This isn't a diet, this is a lifestyle. Eating only one meal a day is not strict, it's very natural. Your one meal a day should be breakfast, literally "break-fast", you're breaking your fast. No, it doesn't have to be in the morning, if anything we recommend against that. Ideally enjoy your meal later in the day at a time that is most convenient for you. If you plan to go eat with friends or family for dinner, then just wait until then. It really is simple. It should always be simple. If removing meat is difficult at first, then start by limiting it to a few days per week. Then, progress to eating meat only one day a week. And before long you'll realize you don't need it, and you're better off without it. Both your physical and spiritual body will certainly thank you for it. Now to really help get you started on this lifestyle journey we have come up with a challenge. The challenge is called the "EZ-28". Because it really is quite easy, and it lasts 28 days long. If you can do something for one month, then you can do it forever. It takes that short amount of time to rewire our brains. And why not rewire your brain to set yourself up for the best version of you for the rest of your life? What are you waiting for? There's no better time to start than right now.

EZ-28 Challenge:

- Start by breaking it up into 4 groups of 7 days.
- For the first 6 days of each group (or week) only eat 1 meal a day. Preferably fruit and/or vegetable based. The easiest time is usually close to or before the usual dinner time so that you will be completely full all the way up until bed and not be tempted to snack.
- On the 7th or last day of the group/week, fast either with only water, or completely dry without food or water, for 24 full hours. (Do not smoke, vape, etc. ONLY water, or if dry fasting literally nothing should go into your mouth, for the full 24 hours.)
- (So the moment after you finish your last bite of food on the 6th day, begin the 24 hour timer.)
- After the 24 hours have ended, break your fast with an enjoyable meal and resume 1 meal a day for the next 6 days. Repeat 3 more times for a total of 4 weeks (28 days)

- Exercise at least 3 days out of the 7 every week. This can be as simple as swimming, playing a sport, biking, dancing, weight training (or just body weight if you fancy that), a martial art, etc. Even just going for a walk in nature, if that's where you feel you need to start. Just be active. Enjoy life.
- This should go without saying, but absolutely zero alcohol.

That's basically all there is to the challenge. It's really quite simple, but the health benefits are enormous. This isn't a diet. This is to help foster a lifestyle that you can continue for the rest of your life. You can do it. What do you have to lose? If you decide it's not for you after completing the challenge, then at the very least you've probably at least lost one thing, a little unwanted weight. And what you can't visibly see is your body getting a chance to remove some of the toxins that have been building up inside your body your whole life. A chance for your organs to heal. A chance for your whole body to regenerate. This "challenge" is a lifestyle that we ourselves live by every single month of the year. It is important to walk the walk, not just talk the talk; and we do just that, because we hold ourselves to a higher standard, and you should as well. You deserve to heal, we all deserve to heal and live the very best life.

APPENDIX: How to 4-day Dry Fast

So, we will just assume a 96 hour, 4 day, dry fast for example. You can feel free to go longer, but once again 4 days is really the minimum you want to strive for. To begin, plan almost a full month to perform this, it is not a quick process, even though the 4 days of dry fasting is quite short, you do not want to skimp out on the preparation and tapering when coming out. The first 2 weeks should be used as preparation. The very first week you should be eating only fruits and drinking water, so that is the very first 7 days. The 2nd week of preparation should consist of the first 5 days (technically days 8-12) consuming only fruit juice, so ideally get a fruit juicer and just juice the fruits yourself. The final 2 remaining days of the 2nd week (days 13-14) should consist of only drinking water, absolutely nothing else. No vaping, no smoking, nothing that your body has to break down other than just water. Now, at this point the dry fast is safe to perform because you have prepared your body properly. Choose a time to begin that works easiest for you, likely sometime in the morning, because on the morning of the 4th day you will be quite happy it ends early in the day, because your lips will be so dry, have no spit in your mouth, and you will be craving the wonderful taste of water. This is a time of healing of not just your physical, but your mental, and spiritual aspects. So, you can really capitalize on that by doing certain things on each day of the fast. First, just for the 4 day dry fast, it may be easiest to go to a place, something like an AirBnB, where you can be away from your regular lifestyle and likely have no options of food and water present to tempt you. Additionally, take this time to take a break from the constant phone usage, video gaming, and show watching that we all so often do daily. Perhaps even bring a book with you. You may watch a show or two before bed, but remove everything else, especially the phone. You will find that without eating and drinking, you have a lot of time on your hands during this fast. This is great, you can finally go back through your life and think about all the things you've just put on the back-burner because our life is full of so many distractions. Every day of the fast, you should try to meditate. You may use your phone for just this exception, but just simply search up a quick 10-20 minute meditation video and follow along. If you've never meditated before, this will be your introduction, and what better time when you have all the time in the world and your focus is on healing yourself. If you're experienced in this, then just meditate however feels right to you, there is no wrong or right way to meditate. You will also find that you don't need much sleep, our bodies use so much energy to digest food and drink that when you eliminate them you will find that you don't actually need to sleep much. In our experience we literally slept for roughly 1 hour each night, not that we wanted to, but after an hour we were just full of energy and could not sleep anymore. So, that's even more time to think, and deal with your own life without having constant dopamine via distractions. One thing to add as well, if you are really feeling a dire thirst, go take a nice shower, you may find yourself taking more than one a day during this fast. But, just remember it's really all just inside your head. Also, don't worry about brushing your teeth, the average person swallows around 5% of the toothpaste whenever brushing, so you don't want to compromise the hard work of your dry fast with something as small as brushing your teeth, especially when you're not even eating anything to dirty them. On day 1 of the dry fast, just focus on getting through the day, the time you begin at counts as the 24 hour mark, in case that wasn't obvious (so if you began at 8am, day 2 starts at 8am on the 2nd day). The reason we make a point to note this is because as soon as day 2 begins, you want to begin a shortened form of Vipassana meditation. What this means, is for the next 12 hours of day 2 you want to be completely silent. Absolutely zero speaking from your mouth. This may seem extreme, but it's something we take for granted in our lives, and even something as short as a 12 hour silence provides an even better chance to think more deeply about your own life and how all of your decisions got you to the exact point you are now. The 2nd day will also be the most difficult to endure, but just know that it really does get much easier after that hurdle, the remaining 2 days will seem much easier in comparison. On the 3rd day, at your leisure, you will want to perform the Ho'oponopono. What this means is to take some paper, possibly a journal, and write down the name of every single person that you have ever met or that has affected your life in some way, either good or bad, line by line. You may need more than 1 or 2 sheets of paper for this. Once you have finished that, then go name by name and thank that person for their effect on your life, because once again, if it were not for them then you wouldn't be at this point. In addition to thanking them, apologize to them for any ill-will you may have towards them, and lastly forgive them for whatever they have done. This may not seem like much to you on the surface, but this is a way of clearing spiritual ties that you may be holding onto subconsciously. Holding onto them does not serve you, and this is another way of cleansing your temple. Whether they forgive you or not, that is not for you to control, you can only control yourself. Finally, on the 4th and final day of the dry fast, you will want to perform a water ceremony. Place the water that you will be breaking your dry fast with on some sort of platform, and then go gather some natural items from around the area like leaves, flowers, branches, or rocks, and build a sort of respectful shrine to commemorate your achievement, and instill appreciation and love for water on a whole new higher level. This is also where you will want to bless the water and instill good intentions into it, just like how it was explained in the prior paragraphs by simple words with your attention. Ideally you can even purchase some small (8oz) blue glass bottles for this. The blue glass also raises the frequency of the water. The size of the container is important as well, that is why around an 8oz size is recommended. Because, of course you will be thirsty and want to guzzle down as much water as you can once having broken the fast. But, there must be one last small stage of discipline exhibited for the next 2 hours of having broken the fast, because your body has been without water for such an extremely long period of time compared to never having been more than a day without water in the rest of your life, it will need a small adjustment phase. So, after having broken your fast with the initial 8oz of water. For the next 2 hours only, consume at most another 8oz of water every 30 minutes in 30 minute intervals. So that's a total of 32oz of water for the next 2 hours in 4 different intervals of 30 minutes each. Once you have finally finished that last 2 hour hurdle, feel free to drink water to your heart's content. Now that your dry fast is over, it is still important to be careful re-adjusting back to solid foods. So, for the next 2 days (48 hours), only consume nothing but water. After those 2 days of re-adjusting with only water, for the next 3 days (72 hours) minimum, only consume fruit juice. Finally, now that it's been 5 total days since ending your dry fast, you can begin again to eat solid foods. Stick to water-dense fruits (oranges, watermelon, grapes, apples, etc.) for at least the next 2 days (48 hours), and then after that you can move back to regular life and enjoy more regular foods. Thus completing a 7 day re-adjustment phase after ending your dry fast. In total this should have taken roughly 25 days to complete, 2 weeks prep, 4 days fasted, and 1 week afterwards to re-adjust. You will notice that your stomach has shrunken quite a bit, and likely you've lost quite a bit of weight. Use this to your advantage, not only has your body now reset its deep water with fresh new high frequency water, but it's also had an enormous time to do a lot of healing and removing of built-up plaque in your body. Especially mucoid plaque, which is the combination of mucus and food residue that coats the gastrointestinal tract.

Audric (left) and Otto (right) are two brothers from the deep south of Louisiana. Audric dropped out of university and is an Air Force veteran as a cybersecurity specialist, and a practitioner of jiu jitsu for many years. Otto attended community college for hairdressing and has been actively pursuing a career in golf for over a decade.. They are just two regular brothers who spent years reading ancient texts and books to understand the wisdom of the ancients because they saw too many inconsistencies with the world around them and wanted to help fix it.